Hurricane Special

Maurice Allward

LONDON
IAN ALLAN LTD

First published 1975

ISBN 0 7110 0541 9

Paintings by M. Roffe

Published by Ian Allan Ltd, Shepperton, Surrey,
and printed in the United Kingdom by
Biddles Ltd, Guildford, Surrey.

ACKNOWLEDGEMENTS

I wish to thank all the many people who have provided
help and encouragement without whose assistance
Hurricane Special would not have been produced.

As photographs are a vital part of the book, special
thanks are due to Mr. E. Hine of the Imperial War
Museum, Dick Richardson of the Strathallan Aircraft
Collection, John Taylor, Flight International and many
others for their help in providing these.

I also thank Philip Lucas, John Scott, Maurice
Crampton and J. V. Tonge for supplying anecdotes which
I am sure have enhanced the interest of the book.

Special thanks are due to Humphrey Wynn and Teddy
Haslam of the Air Historical Branch (RAF) Ministry of
Defence, and particularly to air historian Ted Hooton, for
supplying me with the records and basic statistics used to
prepare my analysis of the events of September 15th, 1940
in Battle of Britain Postscript.

In some instances companies from whom assistance
was requested were either unable or unwilling to provide
information. In such cases my sincere thanks are offered
to individuals. Thank yous are thus gratefully offered to
Sir Harry Broadhurst and Jack Collings of Hawker
Siddeley Aviation, Kingston.

It is also a pity that the Russian authorities were
unable to provide from their extensive archives any new
photographs of some of the many Hurricanes with which
they were supplied at so great a cost in both materials and
men.

Contents

Title page: The Hurricane MkIIA, Series 2, was powered by a Rolls-Royce Merlin XX engine developing 1,300bhp at take-off at sea level, and giving a top speed of 342mph at 17,500ft.
Introduced on the production lines toward the end of October, 1940, this version was armed with eight 0.303in Browning machine-guns instead of the originally-planned twelve, in view of an anticipated shortage of Browning guns during the Battle of Britain, which in the event never materialised.

Left: 'The Grim Reaper' was the insignia on a Hurricane MkIIA, Series 2, used for the local defence of the great Hawker factory at Parlaunt Farm, Langley, in Buckinghamshire. This factory, expressly built for the purpose of manufacturing Hurricanes, was to produce over 7,000 of the fighters during the World War II.

Above: Hurricane MkIV prototype, with additional armour and tropical filter fitted, but no external armament or stores. Powered by a Rolls-Royce Merlin 32 with a Spitfire-type Rotol four-blade propeller, this first flew on March, 14th 1943, at the hands of Philip Lucas. The aircraft was similar to the MkIIC, but with 'universal armament' wings capable of carrying a wide variety of stores. These wings, together with the additional armour protection, resulted in a heavier aircraft and thus reduced performance. Production MkIVs had a 1,620bhp Merlin 24 or 27, with three-blade propellers. The second prototype MkIV, KZ 193, was initially powered by a Merlin 27 but this was replaced by a ground-boosted Merlin 32 driving a Spitfire-type Rotol four-blade propeller to become the prototype MkV. Developing around 1,700bhp at sea level, this powerplant gave a top speed of 326mph with tropical filter and 40mm anti-tank guns. However, severe overheating shortened the engine life, and the ground-boosting aspect was abandoned.

Portrait of a Fighter

The Hurricane was not the fastest fighter of its day. It did not bear the heaviest armament. Its main adversary could out-dive it. Its method of construction was not as advanced as that of some of its contemporaries.

The Hurricane was, however, the right fighter, in the right place, at the right time—in *sufficient quantities*. Just.

Without the Hurricane—and of course its immortal pilots and radiolocation (radar)—the vital Battle of Britain would almost certainly have been lost, and with it the war—and democracy. Let there be no misunderstanding about this basic fundamental fact.

When approached from the ground the Hurricane had a definite purposeful appearance. Although not so 'streamlined' as the Spitfire, it was by no means an ugly aeroplane. Its lines compared well with those of the Messerschmitt Bf109, and with its French, Italian and American and Russian contemporaries. Its rather 'hefty' proportions were just right for a fighter, and gave the impression that here was an aircraft that could dish out—and absorb—punishment.

The cockpit was roomy, and although the layout of the various instruments, controls and switches may look a little untidy to our more sophisticated eyes today, particularly because of the exposed plumbing, it was average for its day and occasioned no undue praise or criticism.

With regard to the armament, the cone of fire from the eight 0.303in. rifle-calibre Browning machine-guns was quite devastating, at the point of convergence, against the lightly armoured German aircraft during the first crucial year of the war. This was particularly so after the introduction of de Wilde ammunition early in 1940. This was a new incendiary that had a very slight delay in the fuse which allowed the bullet to penetrate before breaking up and becoming 'incendiary.'

The Hurricane was an exceptionally stable gun platform, and the close spacing of the guns relative to the centre-line gave the aircraft a deeper 'focus' of fire than had the Spitfire. The close spacing of the guns also lessened the reduction in effectiveness of the armament when the average pilot tended to open fire at too great a range.

Admittedly, the light calibre of the armament meant that accurate aiming was required in oblique attacks for these to be effective. Some pilots would have preferred 20mm cannon, which could be fired effectively from 500-800 yards. However, the installation of these heavy weapons detracted significantly from the Hurricane's performance and their availability during the Battle of Britain, when the fighter was used for interception, on balance would probably have been detrimental. Later on, of course, cannon helped to give the Hurricane a new lease of life for ground attack operations.

In the air the Hurricane was very much a pilot's aeroplane. No effort had been spared to ensure that it was as simple and easy to fly as possible. True, the ailerons tended to become a little heavy at speed—but this was a characteristic common to many of its contemporaries. It was a very forgiving aircraft, more so than the Spitfire. This gave young pilots confidence, particularly in the vital early stages of their careers.

The wide track undercarriage and low pressure tyres, features embodied at the special insistence of Sydney Camm, not only permitted operations from really rough landing strips, but gave added margins of safety during take-off and landing. Later on the robust landing gear was a major factor contributing to the Hurricane's success in the ground attack role as it permitted the carriage of a great weight of under-wing armament.

The Hurricane's 'less advanced' method of construction made it an easier aeroplane to build than the Spitfire—and to repair. The significance of this cannot be over emphasised. It is one of the factors which made the Hurricane the 'best' fighter at the time it was most needed.

An indication of the relative ease with which the Hurricane could be built is given by the Harrogate Programme. Laid down in January 1940, this called for the production of 1,769 fighters during the next seven months, of which 1,045 were to be Hurricanes. In the event, 2,317 fighters were built, of which 1,373 were Hurricanes. The additional 328 Hurricanes represented 60% of the extra fighters produced.

The age old controversy of 'how good was the Hurricane compared with this or that aeroplane' will never be resolved completely as it is undefinable in precise terms. An indication of how certain basic performance parameters compared with those of its chief adversary, the Messerschmitt Bf109, was given when, on May 2nd, 1940 a Bf109E was forced down, undamaged, near Amiens in France. It was immediately inspected and flown by pilots

Above: Hurricane MkIV armed with eight 60lb rockets under the wings. As destructive as a broadside from a naval destroyer, these weapons wrought great execution against ground targets and enemy shipping during the last two years of the war.

Left: Hurricane MkIIC in typical daily war paint.

of No 1 (F) Squadron and assessed against their own Hurricanes.

The pilots' verdict was that, when fitted with a constant-speed propeller, the Hurricane was much more manoeuvrable at all altitudes and actually faster at ground level. The Bf109 was considered to be faster at its rated altitude and, surprisingly, to have a better field of view. This latter comment was probably true for that particular aircraft, as it did not have the rather restrictive armour plate behind the pilot's head which was fitted later.

Two days later the Bf109 was flown to the Aircraft and Armament Experimental Establishment at Boscombe Down for a more scientific assessment of its performance.

The official testing, however, indicated that the Hurricane, even when fitted with a constant-speed propeller, was inferior to the German fighter in all performance respects with the exception of low-altitude manoeuvrability and turning circles at all altitudes. The German fighter was marginally faster at most altitudes and, being fitted with direct fuel injection, could easily out-dive the Hurricane. Its rate of roll was also superior.

In view of this it is somewhat surprising that the Hurricane did as well as it did in combat against the Bf109E. (It was, of course, completely outclassed by the BfG and BfF.) This was achieved by tactics and by utilising the advantages it had to the full.

The most important of these was undoubtedly its superior rate of turn. The official assessment that the Hurricane was 'inferior' to the German fighter in all performance respects with the exception of low-altitude manoeuvrability and turning circles at all altitudes could have been rephrased with advantage as 'the Hurricane's overall manoeuvrability was superior at low altitude, and it could out-turn the German fighter at all altitudes.' This ability was usually enhanced by the tendency of many pilots to use the engine boost override continually during interceptions, a practice which the Merlin engine withstood remarkably well.

This would have put the emphasis on what is undoubtedly a key requirement for a successful fighter—a high rate of turn. Regarding this, it has been claimed that the Hurricane could out-turn any of its contemporaries, with the exception of Japan's Zero.

In the *recorded* instances when Hurricane and Bf109 engaged in individual combat, the German machine was the victor more often than was the Hurricane. One should not, however, dwell too much on the Hurricane's ability to master the Messerschmitt fighter. During the vital Battle of Britain its main targets were German bombers, not fighters. Against the bombers it was deadly.

One cause of some confusion is the maximum speed of the 'Battle of Britain' Mark 1 Hurricanes, powered by Merlin engines fitted with three-blade, variable pitch propellers.

Official flight test records show that new machines off the production line had maximum speeds ranging from 320mph to 328mph, the variation being accounted for by the different degrees of skill available during the finishing stages. Lord Dowding is widely remembered for quoting a maximum speed of 305mph, but this undoubtedly referred to a repaired aircraft, and a pretty battle-scared one at that.

The robustness of the Hurricane and its ability to withstand battle damage is legendary. Time and time again Hurricanes returned from interception sorties with parts of the main structure shot away, with control surfaces almost useless, and with holes in the wing and fuselage large enough for a man to crawl through.

One pilot brought his Hurricane back with one of the aileron hinges shot away and all the controls damaged in some way or another. During the Battle of France one pilot flew his Hurricane safely back to Britain with three of the four main fuselage longerons completely broken and temporarily repaired with wooden splints.

The author personally recalls the occasion when one Hurricane flew into a balloon cable which cut right through the front spar and the two sub-spars in the wing. The cable was half way through the rear spar when the wire broke, and the Hurricane returned to base with the outer wing panel attached by one severely damaged spar!

During one encounter a Hurricane hit another aircraft head on, and fell to the earth with the pilot strapped in the cockpit. The damaged aircraft landed upside down—with the pilot alive—the cockpit surviving the impact because of the strength afforded by the armour plate behind the seat.

During a genuinely low-level attack against an anti-aircraft gun one Hurricane pilot removed the top

layer of sandbags protecting the gun with his wing tip, then flew into and cut a high tension wire, and returned to base.

While recording these examples of the Hurricane's robustness, it is not forgotten that it was the pilots who actually demonstrated the robustness. This was plainly evident in an official Air Ministry Bulletin issued in May, 1940:

'The aircraft was severely damaged before the pilot left on his journey home. The gun-sights were gone and the only instruments working were his compass, and oil temperature and pressure gauges. He had no incendiary or tracer ammunition, and his eight machine-guns were loaded with ordinary ammunition. The pilot was concerned chiefly about the starboard petrol tank, which was leaking. He therefore decided to land at an aerodrome in Northern France to refuel before continuing his flight to England. When he was approaching the aerodrome he saw that part of the town nearby was in flames, and just as he was preparing to come down from 5,000feet he observed two Dornier 215s going in to attack the aerodrome. Immediately he got on the tail of one of them and gave it two short bursts. There was no doubt he hit the enemy aircraft, although he had no gun-sight. The second German machine tried to escape in the clouds, but the Hurricane pilot followed him, blazing away with his guns. Having got rid of the two Dorniers, the New Zealander was about to land when he was attacked by a number of

Left: P Z865, the last of over 14,000 Hurricanes built and appropriately named 'The Last of the Many', displays its fine lines against a peaceful cloud backdrop. Its shape differs little from that of the prototype completed nine years earlier.

Below: Hurricanes took good care of you. Directional control was presumably a little coarse on this Hurricane which flew 36 miles safely back to its base after being shot-up in November 1940. / PNA photo.

Messerschmitt fighters. Unable to cope with all of them immediately, he circled the town for about ten minutes, giving them occasional bursts. When he landed at the aerodrome he found that his starboard tank was spurting petrol. The men on the ground refused to fill his tank, saying that it would be suicide to go up in that machine, so the pilot had to compromise. He had his port tank fuelled, and with a bayonet widened the holes in the punctured tank to allow the fuel to escape. Then he took off again, although he had only fifty rounds left in each of his eight machine-guns. "With only that small amount of ammunition I was almost helpless," he said later, "it was just my luck to run into another formation of six Messerschmitts when I was practically out of petrol. Anyway I gave the leader a burst as he came head on for me. I'm sure I hit him, and I dived down past him towards the ground. After that I just put my skates on for home. It was good fun that fight, but what would I have given for more ammunition to deal with the Messerschmitts.'"

After the encounter the Hurricane was examined when numerous bullet holes were found in the wings, fuselage and tail.

This particular Hurricane was decorated with a 'coat of arms' designed by the pilot himself. The middle comprised a large figure 13. Around this were sketches depicting a broken mirror, a man walking under a ladder, and one showing three cigarettes being lighted with one match. Underneath were the words 'What the Hell.'

First of the Many

The first drawings of the Hurricane were issued to the workshops on November 17th, 1934, but the genesis of the aircraft begins several years before this. . . .

The first twinkling came in January, 1930, when No 33 Squadron was issued with the new Hawker Hart, two-seat light day bomber. It had a top speed of 184mph and was able to outstrip the RAF's Home Defence Siskin fighters in the Air Exercises that year. The writing was beginning to appear on the wall for biplane fighters.

In 1933 Hawkers redressed the bomber/fighter situation with the introduction of the Fury single-seat interceptor fighter. This elegant biplane, with a maximum speed of 207mph, was the first fighter in any air force to exceed 200mph, and the Mark II version was the first to exceed 250mph.

It was, however, apparent to Sydney Camm and his design team that the Fury was not the last word in fighter evolution—it was the last biplane. The speed margin of the Fury of a little more than 20mph over the Hart was obviously no more than a stopgap solution. Accordingly, thought was given to means of increasing the fighter's most significant feature, its speed. In August, 1933, Sydney Camm conferred with the Air Ministry on the subject of future fighter requirements, and referred to a possible monoplane development of the Fury. The Air Ministry indicated its interest.

At that time no drawings existed but two months later an initial design had been evolved as a private venture. Known as the Fury Monoplane, this was a graceful single-seat fighter, armed with four machine-guns, powered by a Rolls-Royce Goshawk steam-cooled in-line engine, and having a fixed, single-strut spatted undercarriage. The fuselage was, as might be expected, similar to that of the High Speed Fury. One notable feature was the neat fairing enclosing the cockpit, providing the pilot with excellent visibility. A large radiator was located under the front of the wing. The wings were relatively thick cantilever members, with slightly tapered leading and trailing edges. The tail surfaces, at this early stage, were almost identical to those on the Fury.

It is of interest to note that while the Hawker design team were evolving the Fury Monoplane, they also found time to produce proposals for twenty-six variations of the Hart and twelve new versions of the Fury, a tender for a light day bomber, and another tender for a four-gun fighter biplane. This latter, the PV3, was produced to meet Air Ministry Specification F7/30, requiring improvements in all the major facets of fighter design—in speed, in rate of climb, in ceiling, in manoeuvrability and firepower. A top speed of 250mph was optimistically requested. This most-demanding Specification was initiated in 1930, but as its achievement depended upon a powerplant which had not then been developed, little

progress was made towards meeting the requirements. By 1933, however, engine advances were such that Hawkers were confident that their biplane, powered by a Rolls-Royce Goshawk, would meet the Specification. It was obvious, however, that the Fury Monoplane, which held promise of a speed some 25mph greater than that of the biplane, was the better project. The passage of time had overtaken the 'advanced' Specification F7/30.

In January, 1934, the Fury monoplane design was altered to accommodate the new Rolls-Royce PV12 engine. This was more powerful than the Goshawk and used a more conventional liquid-cooling system. The new engine was flight tested in two Hawker Horsleys, the High Speed Fury and a Hart. The experience so gained proved invaluable in developing the new engine installation on the monoplane project. The new engine was slightly heavier than the Goshawk and to redress the centre of gravity problem the radiator was moved aft about 18 inches. At this stage the Fury Monoplane—or rather the 'Interceptor Monoplane' as it was now referred to—was still envisaged as having a fixed undercarriage. By 1934, however, a number of American combat aircraft were appearing with retractable undercarriages and an investigation was put in hand to see if one could be evolved for the Interceptor Monoplane. The movement of the radiator aft left the empty front spar centre-section bay fortuitously unobstructed, but the detail design of the undercarriage did not prove easy. To make use of the empty bay, and to provide the wide track insisted upon by Camm, dictated inward-retracting legs. Weight distribution, however, required that the legs be mounted close to the front spar and canted well forward. The resultant geometry made it necessary to embody a break in the side strut so that, during retraction, the leg moved rearward in order for the wheel to clear the main spar. Although somewhat complicated, the undercarriage was later to establish a well-deserved reputation for strength and reliability.

Above: The prototype K5083 making an early landing, as is evident from the original single-frame canopy and the wheel flaps.

Above right: The prototype fuselage under construction. The traditional Hawker structure of wire-braced tubular struts is plainly evident in this view. It was strong yet light, simple to build and easy to repair.

Below: Although it was a simple aeroplane by current standards, the Hurricane had its own complexities as is apparent from this photograph of the engine installation. The word 'monoplane' on this early print is of interest. Other early photographs are labelled Interceptor Monoplane. The name Hurricane was not allocated until June 1936.

Right: Main undercarriage leg fairing and wheel flap. During an early taxying trial over uneven ground the wheel flaps were damaged slightly and subsequently removed permanently. Apart from this minor mishap, the retractable under-carriage, which was something of an innovation at the time, received compliments for its strength and reliability.

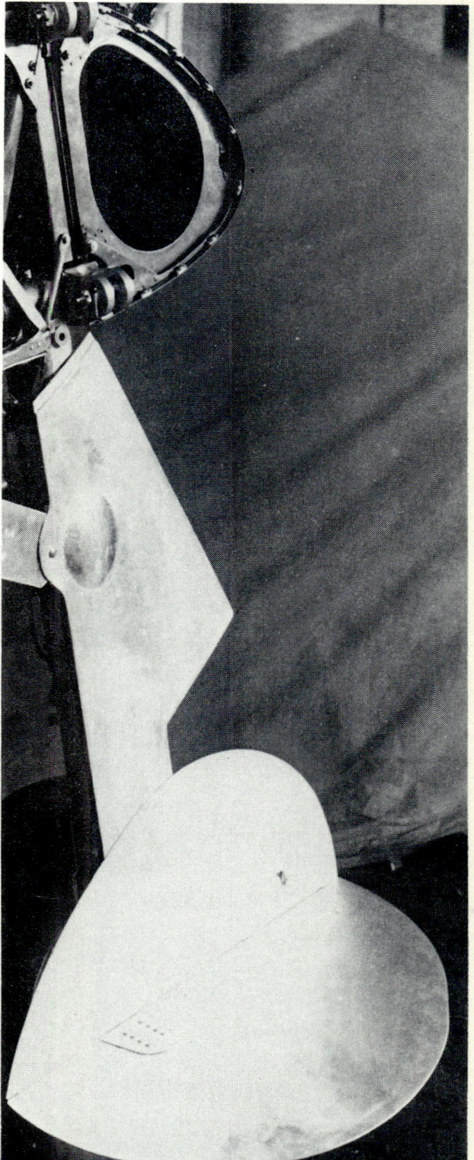

At this stage the armament, influenced by Specification F7/30, consisted of two fuselage-mounted Vickers guns and two wing-mounted Browning guns. The evolution of the armament of the Hurricane is a story in itself and is described later on in this book. Briefly, however, four guns were already known to be inadequate and in the early months of 1934 the Hawker team considered ways of adapting the Interceptor Monoplane— still a private venture—to meet a new Air Ministry Specification F5/34 calling for no less than eight guns.

A small wind tunnel model of the aircraft was built in June, 1934, and in August this was satisfactorily 'flown' at speeds equivalent to 350mph without any aerodynamic vices appearing. The aircraft, it was estimated, would actually have a maximum speed of about 320mph at about 15,000ft.

It was becoming increasingly obvious that the Hawker Private Venture was an interceptor of unusual potential and to formalise the situation the Air Ministry drew up a special Specification, F36/34, titled 'Single-Seat Fighter—High Speed Monoplane,' calling up all the basic features and estimates of the Hawker project. Hawkers then officially 'tendered' their Private Venture on September 4th, 1934. Not surprisingly this was accepted and less than six weeks later the first drawings of the fuselage were issued. In December a wooden mock-up was made to help the detail design of the cockpit instrumentation, pilot's windscreen and canopy, the armament installation, coolant ducting and the undercarriage retraction geometry. December also saw the engine position clarified. Rolls-Royce were confident that their new engine would develop 1,025hp at take off for an installed weight of less than 1,200lb. The power/weight ratio of 0.85 was very advanced for an engine at that time.

With the engine output finalised Hawkers prepared revised performance figures in February, 1935. The new fighter, these indicated, would have a maximum speed in level flight of 330mph at 15,000ft. The service ceiling was 32,500ft and the landing speed just over 70mph.

On February 21st, 1935, Hawkers received a contract—for one prototype. Work on the new aircraft proceeded apace at the Canbury Park Road works in Kingston-on-Thames during the summer of 1935. By August the machine was structurally complete, and the engine—now known as the Merlin—installed. On October 23rd the prototype was taken from Kingston to the Hawker assembly shop at Brooklands where it was re-assembled and tested. On November 6th, 1935, George Bullman made a few acclimatising taxy runs. Satisfied, he opened up to full power and the silver painted monoplane, registered K5083, accelerated down the runway and took off. The first of the many had flown.

As might be expected, with such an advanced machine, a number of problems revealed themselves during its flying trials. Engine troubles necessitated several engine changes. The cockpit canopy was stiffened and the radiator enlarged. The tailplane bracing strut was removed as were the small wheel flaps which tended to get damaged when taxying over rough ground. The problems, however, were of a relatively minor nature and within

three months of its first flight, the aircraft was delivered to the Aircraft and Armament Experimental Establishment, at Martlesham Heath, for its initial evaluation by the Royal Air Force.

The trials were passed without serious trouble. Points commented on favourably included the cockpit, the general view, particularly during take-off and landing, and the undercarriage. About the only adverse comment concerned the aileron and rudder controls, which became rather heavy at high speed.

After the trials, K5083 returned to Brooklands where the normal development flying continued.

At this stage international events, including the Italian invasion of Abyssinia, influenced the Hawker board of directors to order the start of the preparation of production drawings, although no official order had been received at that time. The Hawker planning department was instructed to prepare schedules catering for a potential output of no less than one thousand machines. Once again Hawker initiative was rewarded and, on June 3rd, 1936, the Air Ministry awarded the company a contract for six hundred aircraft. Just over three weeks later, on June 27th, the Air Ministry officially approved the name Hurricane.

In September it was decided that the Merlin I, which powered the prototype, would not be put into production.

Above: The prototype at Brooklands shortly before its second move to Martlesham Heath. The strut bracing the tailplane has been removed, and the canopy strengthened by an additional frame. Internally, the radio has been installed.

Left: A fine air view of the Hurricane prototype. In this view the canopy has been strengthened, but the tailplane is still braced. Note also the retractable tailwheel; this feature was deleted on production aircraft. The opinion of the French magazine 'Les Ailes' of the new British fighter was: 'The Hurricane is an experimental speed aeroplane and not a truly military aircraft'.

Below: The first production Hurricane I, L1547. Of interest are the early 'kidney' exhaust stubs, the two-blade wooden propeller, and the absence of the under-fin anti-spin fairing. The aircraft was built at Kingston and taken by road to Brooklands for final assembly, weighing and engine running. It first flew on October 12th 1937 at the hands of test pilot Philip Lucas.

Bottom: Hurricane I, L1606, previously one of No 56 Squadron's aircraft, was purchased back from the Air Ministry by Hawkers for propeller trials. Company registered G-AFKX, a Merlin III, with a standardised propeller shaft capable of accommodating either Rotol or de Havilland propellers, was installed and a Rotol all-metal, three-blade constant speed wide-pitch-range propeller fitted. Although some 300lb heavier than the two-blade propeller, this and the de Havilland Hamilton two-pitch, three-blade propeller, resulted in a significant increase in climb performance, reducing the time to the rated altitude by over a minute. Later G-AFKX was used to test the all-metal wings and the TR 1133 radio installation. It was also used as a test bed for the Rolls-Royce RM45 engine (Merlin 45).

Its place would be taken by the improved Merlin G, later known as the Merlin II. The new engine had different rocker boxes which affected the whole shape of the upper nose fairing. Alterations were also made to the air intake, propeller, engine controls, engine mounting. Due to the alterations to the cowling, the glycol tank had to be repositioned. The hand starting system was also improved. These changes delayed production by nearly four months and it was not until October 12th, 1937 that the first production Hurricane, L1547, flew in the capable hands of Hawker test pilot Philip Lucas.

Production Hurricanes embodied several other improvements. The windscreen and cabin top were faired more neatly into the fuselage. New streamlined 'kidney' exhausts were fitted in place of the stub exhausts, and the rudder mass balance was enclosed. Later machines embodied fixed tail-wheels, and a deeper rudder and small ventral fairing to improve the handling in a spin, and serving also to fair in the tailwheel. Rolls-Royce ejector type exhaust stubs resulted in a 2mph speed improvement. Early Hurricanes were fitted with two-blade fixed-pitch wooden propellers but later, as the demand for greater performance became vital, variable-pitch propellers were introduced. First of these was the de Havilland two-position, followed by the de Havilland and Rotol constant-speed propellers.

Squadron Treble One

The first Squadron to receive the Hurricane was No 111 (Fighter) Squadron, based at Northolt. Originally formed in 1917 to combat German fighters and reconnaissance aircraft causing a nuisance over Palestine, the Squadron later achieved the distinction of being one of the select few whose number became widely known among the general public. This was due to its formation of the famous 'Treble One' aerobatic team of black Hawker Hunters in the 1950's.

In 1937 the unit was equipped with Gloster Gauntlets, and the transition to the Hawker monoplane fighter in 1938 involved a jump in top speed of nearly 100mph, while the armament increased from two to eight machine-guns, and, additionally, the pilots were introduced to an enclosed cockpit and a retractable undercarriage. These 'quantum' jumps were viewed with misgiving by some of the less experienced pilots, a view reinforced by a number of landing accidents during the first few weeks, one of which resulted in the loss of the pilot.

To demonstrate to his pilots, and to the general public, the capabilities of the new fighter, the squadron commander, Squadron Leader John Gillan, decided to make a high speed flight from Northolt to Turnhouse, Edinburgh, and return, a round trip of over 650 miles. Making the attempt on February 10th, 1938, Gillan encountered strong headwinds on his flight northwards, and landed late in the day. On the return flight, however, the wind naturally benefited him, and the next morning a startled public learned that the Hurricane had covered the 327 miles at an average speed of 408mph. The energetic tailwind of some 80mph was, not unnaturally, little publicised. Of interest is that during the flight the engine speed remained above 2,950rpm as Gillan used almost take-off boost throughout the flight. This was an early demonstration of the inherent reliability of the Merlin for the overspeeding engine was obviously subjected to much higher stresses than normal.

When war was declared on Germany on September 3rd, 1939, the Squadron dispersed its aircraft, and its 22 pilots waited for the fleets of Luftwaffe bombers to appear, on their way to destroy London. Fortunately, these mass attacks did not materialise. What did materialise were air attacks on British naval units off the South East coast and consequently these were transferred North to Edinburgh. To help counter the resulting German activity against the Navy in the Firth of Forth, No 111 was sent to Acklington in Northumberland in October.

In spite of numerous patrols, a month passed before an enemy aircraft was caught. Then, one very foggy morning, two German reconnaissance aircraft were plotted, but not seen. In an attempt to intercept them an adjacent auxiliary squadron scrambled two Spitfires, both of which crashed, one being fatal. The enemy aircraft were then plotted heading towards the area covered by No 111.

In spite of the bad weather the young squadron commander Squadron Leader Harry Broadhurst, decided to attempt an interception, being prepared to bale out on his return if he was unable to land.

Taking off, in aircraft N2340, Broadhurst climbed through the fog and into the low cloud, and was successfully vectored towards one of the intruders, a Heinkel He111 bomber, about eight miles east of Alnwick. He emerged from the cloud to find the enemy bomber almost above him. As he approached, the German crew spotted the Hurricane and the bomber dived for cloud cover, firing its ventral gun. Broadhurst manoeuvred his Hurricane directly behind the Heinkel and fired several long bursts. The bomber turned first on its side and then started to dive nearly vertically, trailing smoke. The Hurricane had to pull out violently to avoid hitting the water. Seconds later the Heinkel crashed, and No 111 had chalked up the first of its many victories of the war.

The combat was all over in a few minutes and, with almost full fuel tanks, the Hurricane cruised around until ground control were able to guide the pilot to an airfield with sufficient visibility for him to land.

After this episode, Broadhurst went on to achieve high rank in the RAF, and today, as Sir Harry, is a director of Hawker Siddeley.

Above: Hurricanes of No 111 (Fighter) Squadron in close formation. This Squadron was the first unit in the Royal Air Force to be equipped with the Hurricane, deliveries starting in December 1937. It was thus the first squadron in the world to fly an eight-gun monoplane fighter. During the transition from Gloster Gauntlets, the Squadron lost its traditional black bar marking on the fuselage, but mounted the Squadron badge on the fin in the absence of a fin flash.

Right: Hurricanes of No 111 (Fighter) Squadron. Note the absence of the anti-spin fairings under the tails of these two early machines. The nearer of the two, L1550, was the fourth production aircraft.

Above: Hurricanes of No 111 (Fighter)
Squadron lined up at Northolt, the squadron's
base, just after the Munich crisis. This period
saw the introduction of code letters for RAF
aircraft; TM were used until the outbreak of war
in 1939.

Above right: Refuelling a Hurricane of No 111
(Fighter) Squadron at Northolt shortly after its
entry into service.

Right: A 'Treble one' commemorative
photograph taken in 1961 including five of the
aircraft types flown by the Squadron. The
Hurricane, a MkII, is leading a Spitfire Mk19
from the Battle of Britain Flight, a Meteor F8, a
Hunter F6, with a Lightning F1A at the rear.

Their Finest Hours

'What General Weygand called the Battle of France is over. I expect that the Battle of Britain is about to begin. Upon this battle depends the survival of Christian civilization. Upon it depends our own British life and the long continuity of our institutions and our Empire. The whole fury and might of the enemy must very soon be turned on us. Hitler knows that he will have to break us in this island or lose the war.

'If we can stand up to him all Europe may be free and the life of the world may move forward into broad sunlit uplands. But if we fail, then the whole world, including the United States, including all that we have known and cared for, will sink into the abyss of a new dark age, made more sinister and perhaps more protracted by the lights of perverted science.

'Let us therefore brace ourselves to our duties, and so bear ourselves that, if the British Empire and its Commonwealth lasts for a thousand years, men will still say "this was their finest hour."'

Statement by Winston Churchill in the
House of Commons.   June 19, 1940.

For its *Eagle-Attack* on Britain the Luftwaffe massed three great *Luftflotten,* or Air Fleets. One was based in Denmark and Norway, and two in the Low Countries and France.

The combined strength of these fleets was about 2,700 aircraft. Of these 760 were Messerschmitt Bf109s, of which about 670 were serviceable. Over 1,600 bombers were available, of which over 1,300 were long-range twin-engined 'heavy' bombers, the remainder being light Junkers Ju87 dive bombers. The Luftwaffe plan was to shatter the Royal Air Force in a few swift strokes, as it had previously shattered the air forces of Poland and France.

Against this formidable force the Royal Air Force had at its disposal on August 1st, 1940, 48 operational single-engined fighter squadrons. Of these units 27 were equipped with Hurricanes and 19 with Spitfires. The total operational strength of the Hurricane squadrons was 440 aircraft, of which some 332 were serviceable.

In 11 Group, and the adjacent sectors of 10 and 12 Groups, covering the vital south-east corner of England, were 202 serviceable Hurricanes and 99 serviceable Spitfires. This slender force of 301 fighters was soon to determine the fate of Britain. And the world.

The Battle of Britain as it has come to be known has been covered very fully in many other publications and so it will not be described in detail here. It is also emphasised that although, for obvious reasons, attention is focused on exploits of the Hurricane, this does not imply belittlement of the part played by the Spitfire.

The performance of the Hurricane in combat presents something of an enigma. As indicated previously, the Messerschmitt Bf109 was marginally superior to the Hurricane in all respects at most heights, except for rate of turn. There are, however, numerous examples on record of Hurricanes bettering the Messerschmitt' fighter when heavily outnumbered. This is, perhaps, not unexpected as those occasions when it fared badly are unlikely to have been well documented for understandable reasons.

During August and September when the great air battles raged over Southern England almost daily, records exist of 331 'dog fights' in which a Hurricane engaged a Bf109 in individual combat. In these the Bf109 was the victor on 207 occasions and the Hurricane on 124. It must be emphasised that these figures relate only to those combats where the identity of the victor was definitely known, and thus only tell part of the overall story. For example, in September about 178 Bf109s were shot down but for only 88 of them could their adversary be positively identified. The remaining 90 are listed as 'shot down by British fighters over. . . .' Also it has been rumoured that some Luftwaffe fighter pilots, having been bettered by a Hurricane, felt a little ashamed and either reported that they had not identified their attacker—or that it was a Spitfire! On the other hand in a dog fight, the victor of a shot down Hurricane or Spitfire was, inevitably, a Bf109.

Also relevant is the fact that the Bf109s were not the prime targets of either the Hurricane or the Spitfire. The German fighter could not have beaten Britain, but the bombers could, and so these were the prime target. Eleven Group stressed the importance of avoiding fighter-to-fighter combat whenever possible. Even in September, when the Spitfire pilots were specifically instructed to go for the 109s, this was primarily a measure to help shoot down more bombers—by keeping the 109s off the Hurricanes.

Above: August 15th 1940. Two Hurricanes of
No 501 (County of Gloucester) Squadron
scrambling from Gravesend on the Thames
estuary, to help intercept some of the 520
bombers and 1,270 fighters launched against
Britain that day. A record total of 76 German
aircraft were shot down for the loss of 34
Fighter Command aircraft, causing the
Germans to refer to August 15th as 'Schwarzer
Donnerstag' — Black Thursday.
The Luftwaffe Airfleet Luftflotte 5, based in
Denmark and Norway, on this one day alone
lost an eighth of its bombers and a fifth of its
long-range fighters.

Above right: Hurricanes of No 85 Squadron on
patrol.

Right: Czech ground staff service and re-arm a
Hurricane after a heavy encounter with the
enemy.

Because the Hurricane could not effectively pursue a Bf109 if it flick-rolled or dived to break off an engagement, or match it at heights, it was also common sense to direct Hurricane formations against enemy bombers which rarely operated above 17,000ft leaving the Spitfire to tackle the higher-flying escorting fighters. In practice, the small numbers of British fighters available made it difficult to mount such co-ordinated attacks during the first few weeks. In September, when the Luftwaffe eased its attack on fighter stations to bomb London, the concentration on an objective further inland gave more time for the British squadrons to join up in pairs, yet intercept before the Germans reached their intended target.

These tactics completed the undoing of the Luftwaffe. The harassed bombers called for even-closer escort to the extent that the fighters became so tied down they lost all power of initiative and with it much of their ability to defend either themselves or their charges.

At the time of the Battle, the author, then 17 years old and on holiday from school, lived at Whyteleafe, near the important Sector fighter airfield, Kenley, and within 'sight' of the fighter stations at Croydon and Biggin Hill. I kept a daily diary of the times of the air raids. The following entry was written on August 18th, immediately after a heavy raid on Kenley, during which one enemy aircraft seemed to lay a ring of smoke around the airfield, through which other bombers dived to their target. During the attack the ring drifted slowly towards our house. . . .

'We were just finishing dinner when the siren went. We were in the sun parlour, overlooking the airfield, and as usual went outside and peered upwards. We could hear the ominous drone of bombers over the hum of our own Hurricanes and Spitfires.

'Suddenly we saw about 12 of them (bombers) appearing from the sun and diving towards Kenley. Black columns of smoke appeared and we watched, fascinated, still in the open. The ammunition dump was hit, and we were treated to a free firework display. We were so engrossed that we failed to notice another formation of planes appearing from the sun. The first we knew of them was a burst of machine-gun fire from one of our own fighters.

'Suddenly we heard "bang," "bang." As they seemed unpleasantly close we went indoors. . . .'

A detailed account of the Battle records that this was one of the early occasions when sheer weight of numbers enabled an enemy formation of Heinkels and Dorniers to break through, this time to Kenley. In spite of the determined defence afforded by the Hurricanes of No 111 Squadron and Spitfires of No 64 Squadron, the raid destroyed every hangar but one and heavily damaged the runways. And our house!

The Hurricane's main adversary after the Bf109 was its twin-engined stablemate, the Bf110. This fighter tended to operate below 18,000ft and thus was often intercepted by Hurricanes which fared well in combat against this formidable fighter.

The biggest Hurricane—Bf110 engagement occurred on September 4th, appropriately over the Hawker factory

at Brooklands. No 249 and 253 Squadrons, with 22 Hurricanes, were already airborne when they were directed towards the formation of Bf110s, which had broken through the coastal patrols. No 253 Squadron recorded the battle as follows:—

'Kenley, September 4th, 1940. Nine Hurricanes took off from Kenley at 13.05-13.10hrs to patrol base and Croydon at 8,000 feet. They were flying vic formation when they sighted 20 Bf110s about to attack Brooklands aerodrome. Leader turned the formation 90 degrees to starboard and in shallow vic dived to the attack out of the sun from about 12,000 feet. Flt Lt Cambridge, leading the formation, attacked an enemy aircraft from the beam and above, expending all his ammunition in one long burst and saw the target's port engine catch fire. Blue One followed it down and saw it crash in flames in a field. Blue Two (Plt Off Samolinski) attacked another and observed a fire in the cockpit, after which the enemy aircraft turned and went into a dive. Green Two (Sgt Dredge) attacked a Bf110 from thirty degrees above and to the rear, giving a ten second burst while closing from 300 down to 25 yards. Both engines caught fire and a red glow was observed in the cockpit; the enemy was seen to dive straight down and burst into flames (confirmed by Red One). Green Three (Plt Off Novak), after attacking Bf110 observed smoke coming from the fuselage, after which the enemy dived and crashed. Red One (Flt Lt Wedgwood) succeeded in getting on the tail of a Bf110 and fired a ten second burst from 250 yards to point blank range. The enemy caught fire, climbed steeply for a second before falling to crash in a wood. Red Two (Plt Off Corkett) attacked a Bf110 which was flying on the starboard side of the enemy vic; after two bursts the enemy broke formation, climbed 500 feet, turned over on to its back and dived straight down and exploded in a field. Red Three (Sgt Kee) delivered a head-on attack on a Bf110 from slightly below and from 250 yards closing to 50 yards, firing 1-2 second bursts.

Above: Week-end pilots. Auxiliary Air Force personnel of No 601 (City of London) Squadron effecting some rather extensive open-air maintenance in muddy conditions at the edge of their airfield. The aircraft is one of the third production batch of 500 Hawker-built Mark Is.

Above right: Re-arming a Hurricane after a sortie. This was the occasion when, mistaken for Hurricanes by Luftwaffe fighters, turret-armed Defiants claimed to have shot down 37 enemy aircraft in one day, although German records after the war indicated a loss of only 14 aircraft.
During a subsequent patrol the Defiants, accompanied by Hurricanes, shot down a further 12 enemy aircraft.

Centre right: Hurricanes of No 111 Squadron refuelling after a patrol. During the hectic and numerous battles of August and September 1940, pilots were often interrogated by the side of their aircraft while waiting for their next scramble. Also, pilots often landed away from their home base and, with airfields the prime target of the Luftwaffe, communications were usually difficult. These conditions helped give rise to unintentional exaggeration of enemy losses.

Right: Built by the Canadian Car and Foundry Corporation during 1940-41, this MarkI is typical of the Canadian Hurricanes which fought at the end of the Battle of Britain.

Small pieces ripped off the fuselage and tail. Blue Three (Sgt Innes) and Green One (Fg Off Watts) silenced the rear gunners of two Bf110's. Nine Hurricanes landed at Kenley 13.55hrs. Our losses: Nil. Enemy casualties: Six Bf110's destroyed, one damaged.'

So severe was the mauling of this much-vaunted *zerstorer*, operated by Hermann Goering's elite *Zerstorer-geschwader*, that the Marshal had to admit that it was a failure and to allow it to be withdrawn from the Channel coast. But not before the farcical situation had developed in which these twin-engined 'escort' fighters had, in turn, to be escorted by the single-seat Bf109's!

To repair Hurricanes damaged in combat a country-wide repair organisation was set up, involving 25 companies. When a Hurricane was damaged, rather than laboriously transport it back to its parent Hawker factory, it would be taken speedily to the nearest unit in the repair organisation.

The motto of the organisation was 'Keep 'em flying,' and 'red tape' was kept to a minimum. Damage which, according to the official handbook was unrepairable, was referred direct to the Hawker Design Office who, whenever any possible means could be found for restoring the structure to its full strength, immediately designed the necessary special repair scheme. During the vital month of August, 1940, the organisation repaired 107 Hurricanes and during the month of September, 169.

Of the total number of aircraft issued to Fighter Command during the Battle, 65 per cent were new and 35 per cent were repaired aircraft. Of all the Hurricanes that crashed during the Battle, exclusive of missing aircraft which went down off the shores of Britain or over France, 61 per cent are said to have been repaired and put back into service! Of the remaining 39 per cent, many of the wrecks were salvaged and broken down into spare parts to help repair the majority.

When that part of the air war known as the Battle of Britain had ended, German losses totalled 1,607 aircraft, of which 544 were Bf109s. Hurricane and Spitfire losses totalled 818. These figures give a true perspective of the magnitude of the Fighter Command success.

Of interest is the fact that the 'inferior' performance of the Hurricane may have contributed indirectly to the success of the top-scoring No 303 Squadron, flown by Polish pilots, with 62 claimed kills against the Bf109, rather than an above-average 'hatred' for the enemy. Flying definitely inferior equipment in Poland, the pilots had evolved a defensive technique which usually enabled them to evade their superior adversaries. Coming over to Britain they brought their theories with them, which consisted essentially, when an enemy fighter was sighted, of getting down low and flying in a tight circle. As soon as the Polish pilots realised that to try and run from a Bf109 in a Hurricane was to invite being shot down, many tended often to adopt their defensive technique. If the 109 then tried to engage the Hurricane, sooner or later the Hurricane would be on the 109's tail, within firing range!

During the period of the Battle, Hurricanes shot down more aircraft than all other British fighters (obviously primarily the Spitfire) and ground fire combined. As previously indicated, this does not imply the superiority of the Hurricane, but is due to the fact that there were more Hurricanes available than Spitfires. The average totals of serviceable aircraft were 461 and 295 respectively.

What is certain is that without the Hurricane, and its pilots, Britain would have lost the war.

Group	Hurricanes	Spitfires
No. 10		
(Covering South-West England)		
Hurricanes: 3 Squadrons (87, 213, 238)	59	—
Spitfires:　4 Squadrons (92, 152, 234, 609)	—	71
No. 11		
(Covering South-East England)		
Hurricanes: 13 Squadrons (1, 17, 32, 43, 56, 85, 111, 145, 151, 257, 501, 601, 615)	238	—
Spitfires:　6 Squadrons (41/54, 64, 65, 74, 610)	—	100
No. 12		
(Covering mid-England)		
Hurricanes: 5 Squadrons (46, 73, 229, 242, 249)	87	—
Spitfires:　6 Squadrons (19, 66, 222, 266, 611, 616)	—	103
No. 13		
(Covering the North)		
Hurricanes: 8 Squadrons (3, 79, 232(½), 245(NI), 253, 263(½), 504, 605, 607)	143	—
Spitfires:　3 Squadrons (72, 602, 603)	—	47
TOTAL STRENGTH	527	321

LUFTWAFFE STRENGTH ON AUGUST 8th 1940

Luftflotte	Bf109s	Bf110s	Bombers
No. 2			
(Based in Holland, Belgium and N.E. France)	460	90	660
No. 3			
(Based in N.W. France)	300	130	820
No. 5			
(Based in Denmark and Norway)	—	30	130
TOTAL STRENGTH	760	250	1,610

Left: Symbolising the dashed hopes of the
Luftwaffe and the end of the Battle of Britain is
this burning Dornier Do17Z bomber shot down
over the south coast of England.

Hurricane V.C.

Of all the medals awarded for valour, none is more coveted
than Britain's Victoria Cross. This was founded by Queen
Victoria in 1856 as an award open to all ranks in the Army
and Navy without distinction 'who had performed some
signal act of valour.' The creation of other awards
demanding less exacting 'acts of valour' tended to increase
still further the pre-eminence of the Victoria Cross in the
field of military decoration. One result of this is that far
fewer Victoria Crosses were awarded during the Second
World War than during the Great War of 1914-18.

Of the total of 22 V.C.s awarded to the Royal Air
Force during the Second World War, one only was
awarded to a fighter pilot—to the pilot of a Hurricane.

This Victoria Cross was won by Flt Lt James B.
Nicolson of No 249 Squadron, who delayed jumping by
parachute from his blazing Hurricane until he had shot
down a Messerschmitt Bf110 which suddenly came into
his sights. In the process Nicolson suffered excruciatingly
painful burns on his hands.

The sequence of events was as follows. On August 16,
while based at Boscombe Down, No 249 Squadron was
scrambled to patrol between Ringwood and Poole, in the
path of large formations of enemy aircraft then reported to
be crossing the coast. During the patrol, red section, led by
Nicolson, was instructed to investigate a formation of
Bf109s flying over Southampton. On the way to the area
the Section was attacked from behind by a number of
Bf110s. Nicolson was hit almost immediately by four
20mm cannon shells; two shells wounded the pilot himself
and a third struck and ignited the fuel tank just ahead of
the cockpit. Fire at once broke out, fanned by the
slipstream. Nicolson was preparing to bale out when,
through the smoke and flames, he caught sight of a 110
ahead of him, apparently his attacker, which had overshot
him. Although suffering from the two shell wounds, and
sustaining severe burns on his hands, face and legs,
Nicolson remained in his stricken Hurricane long enough
to give the 110 a long burst, causing the enemy fighter to
fall out of control. Only then did Nicolson bale out, to
make a safe but painful parachute descent—and received
the coveted Victoria Cross for his most conspicuous
bravery.

James Nicolson was 23 years old when he won the
award. He recovered from his injuries and eventually
became a Wing Commander. He was lost in an aircraft
that disappeared over the Indian Ocean in 1944.

Right: Flt Lt James B. Nicolson, V.C., No 249 Squadron.

Hurricane Squadrons in Britain 1938 to 1941

The top full line shows the total Hurricane squadrons strength at the first day of each month. The first peak is at September 1st, 1939, with 17½ squadrons (29 Squadron was the ½ squadron with a mixture of Blenheims and Hurricanes).

During September 1939 four squadrons left for France and no more new units were equipped with the Hurricane until February 1940, when the total began to rise. The big jump in July 1940 is due to squadrons returning from France, 46 Squadron being re-formed after Norway and new units being trained.

In September 1940 the first Hurricane night fighter units were formed and these are shown in black hatching. The peak of Hurricane day squadron strength was reached in April 1941 (37 squadrons, all operational). Peak for day and night figher squadrons was January 1941. The sudden drop in May 1941 is due partly to the transfer of units overseas to North Africa, and partly due to some squadrons converting to Spitfires.

The chain dotted line shows *operational* day squadrons of Hurricanes in Britain. Note the dramatic drop to 9½ at June 1st 1940. This is due to sustained operations and fatigue caused by the operations over France and Dunkirk. Of interest is the fact that *every* available Hurricane squadron in the whole of Britain was thrown into the Battle of France and the Dunkirk withdrawal! This factor emphasises Dowding's fears at the time that the transfer of more Hurricanes to France would be disastrous.

This is indicated by the bottom, dotted, line which shows operational day Hurricane squadrons in the South and South East England. At June 1st there were 20½ Hurricane squadrons in Britain—only 9½ of which were operational, with 8½ being in the South of England—leaving only the equivalent of one operational Hurricane squadron (plus 4½ Spitfire squadrons) to cover the entire remaining defence of the country! In other words, no less than 11 squadrons were non-operational after their combat over France prior to June 1st.

Note: South and South East England encompasses 11 Group and Middle Wallop, Warmwell, Boscombe Down, Exeter, Duxford and Coltishall.

The peak of Hurricane squadrons in South/South East England is reached around October 1940 and then declines, as the Spitfire squadrons assume more importance in these sectors. In other words, from October 1940 onwards, the Hurricane was used more for defence in the less hectic areas of the country and also for some night fighting until May 1941 when some had to be spared for North Africa and Malta where the Luftwaffe had appeared in January-February 1941.

Operational units prior to September 1939 are not shown as these are difficult to ascertain. However, at the time of the Munich Crisis there were really only two operational Hurricane squadrons and no Spitfires.

It is a sober thought to recall that *all* the available Hurricane squadrons saw combat between May 10th and June 4th 1940 (15 out of the available 19 Spitfire squadrons did so as well) the period covering the invasion of the Low Countries and the fall of France. This provided wide combat experience for the pilots, but indicates how vulnerable was our state at the time. This full use certainly answers the oft-posed question: 'Where was the Royal Air Force?' They were all there, bar four squadrons.

The graph also shows the astonishing recovery made by the Royal Air Force, between mid-June and August 1940, especially with regard to Hurricane squadrons.

On June 1st there were 20½ Hurricane squadrons and 22 Spitfire squadrons in Britain. By September 1st, there were 34½ Hurricane squadrons to 19 Spitfire squadrons. Thus the production and reserves of the Hurricane was sufficient to allow many new squadrons to be formed in that critical period, whereas Spitfire production could only just keep up with the losses to maintain 19 squadrons until the worst of the Battle of Britain was over.

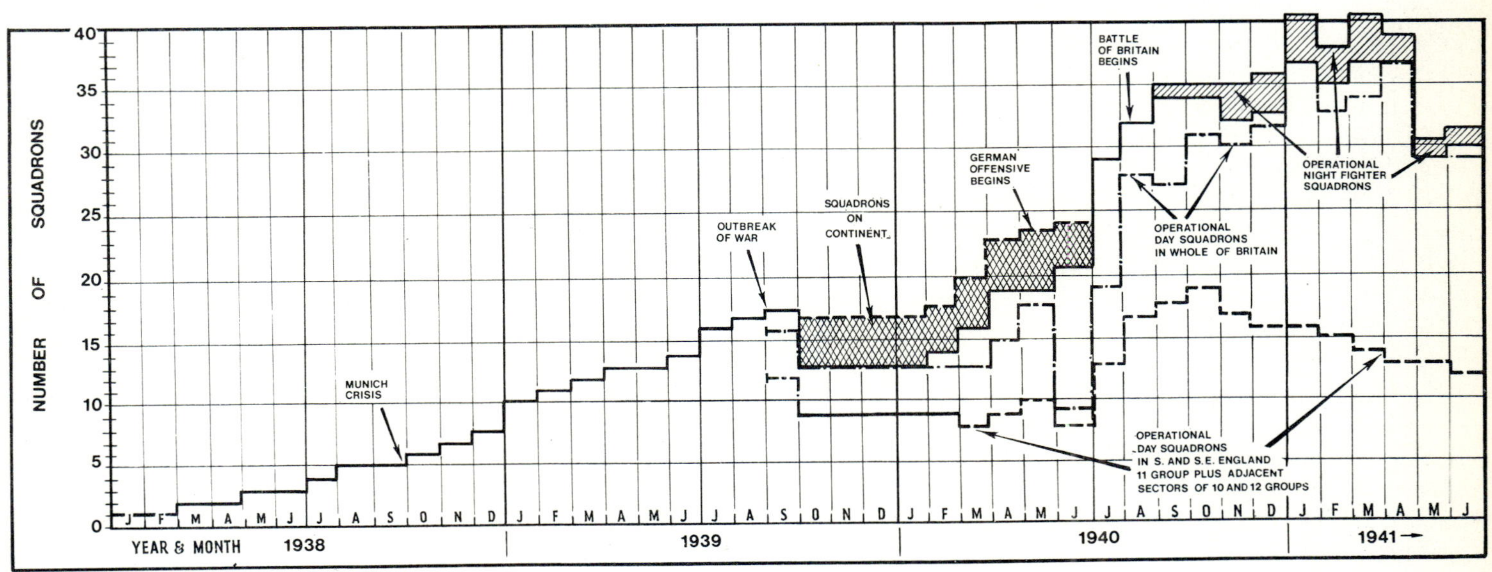

23

Battle of Britain postscript

SEPTEMBER 15, 1940

Wednesday, September 15th, 1940, was the climax of the Battle of Britain. From early in the morning of that mid-September day it was apparent that a major battle was being fought in the blue sky over southern England. As the hours passed by, the estimated number of enemy aircraft shot down increased steadily. By the time the sun had set and the fighting had died down, the total had reached 175. Later that evening, as further reports were received, the total reached 185. Three weeks later, writing in the *War Illustrated* of October 4th, 1940, Air Marshal Sir A. Barratt stated that this figure should be further increased to 232, to embody 47 more 'that almost certainly came down.'

It was, therefore, something of a shock to learn after the war, when captured German documents were examined, that the actual Luftwaffe losses on this key day were not 232, or 185, or even 85 aircraft, but only 54.

When the writer first learned of this revised figure, the initial reaction was one of incredulity. I harboured the deep suspicion that the German records had been tampered with to try and 'downgrade' the importance of the day which Winston Churchill had immortalised as Britain's 'finest hour.' This suspicion was reinforced by the knowledge of the boast of a high ranking German official of his country's ability to re-write events so that the truth would never be known to future generations. There is also contemporary evidence that even established democracies such as the U.K. and the U.S. can withhold facts and truth from most of the people for a long time. To the technical dictatorship of Nazi Germany it would have been even easier.

The German documents referred to are the Quartermaster General Records (6th Department) of the Luftwaffe, listing the replacement aircraft requested. The first losses of September 15th were entered on September 17th and the last ones about a week later. The integrity of these records is considered absolute, both by the Royal Air Force Intelligence and by the custodian of the Bundesarchivis at Breisgau, W. Germany. Commanding officers of units wanting replacements are not likely to minimise their losses. Any clandestine obliteration of entries on instructions from Dr. Goebbels is discounted as this master of mistruth 'had no say in Goering's Luftwaffe.' However, German authorities do concede that 'erroneous entries due to false reports cannot theoretically be excluded,' although no such cases are known.

What is certain is that historians such as Sir Basil Collier, author of 'The Defence of the United Kingdom,' issued by HM Stationery Office in 1957, have officially recorded the German losses that day as 'sixty' aircraft, thus effectively underwriting the figure in the Luftwaffe Quartermaster Records. Francis Mason, who in preparing his book 'Battle over Britain,' went to enormous trouble to check German records and to collate these with Royal Air Force returns and known reports of crashes, detailing what happened to aircraft of both sides, also arrived at a figure of 'sixty' German aircraft lost, again close to the figure in the Bundesarchivis.

What then is the explanation for the great disparity between the figure estimated by the Royal Air Force at the time and that now accepted as the true one? When asking this question one bears in mind the importance of knowing enemy losses accurately and the very strict procedure laid down for pilots to claim a kill, detailed on page 27.

One must also recall how the total, and those for other days, was arrived at. After a big battle there were obvious pressures on the authorities to announce enemy losses as quickly as possible. Thus, a *provisional* total was amassed from many sources, primarily combat reports by pilots, but also from police messages, and coastguard and civilian reports. It was fully appreciated that through unsubstantiated claims and duplication of reports, the total was almost certainly exaggerated. However, it was felt that as, for the first time, the Luftwaffe was being mastered, a little bit of exaggeration wasn't serious and would probably be good for public morale. As far as this latter point is concerned, the writer can confirm that the authorities were absolutely right.

However, the semi-official manner in which the provisional totals were announced by the Air Ministry and the BBC gave them the air of being carefully checked and factual, which they were not, and could not be under the circumstances. This false air of authenticity was much regretted by the Air Ministry and Air Chief Marshal Dowding—but he could do nothing about it, particularly as it proved impossible during the war to assess properly or verify the claims and so arrive at an accurate total. Even after Intelligence had done their best, all Dowding could do was to hazard a guess that the claimed totals were about '25 per cent' too high.

Accepting that the totals were provisional, one might now reasonably ask why even quick estimates should be so far out.

There were three main reasons:

(1) Fighter Command had no experience in assessing claims for aircraft destroyed when large numbers of aircraft were involved. It is now known that the inaccuracy of claims increases in direct proportion to the number of aircraft involved. In really big battles the inaccuracy can reach—and did—300 per cent, or more. This degree of error can also be seen to exist in the claims and actual losses of great ground battles. Thus, September 15th was by no means the only occasion when Royal Air Force victories were grossly exaggerated. For example, on August 15th, when it was estimated that 183 enemy aircraft had been shot down, the real total was 76. On August 18th, 155 were claimed, the actual total being 71; August 31st, claimed: 94, actual 39; September 7th,

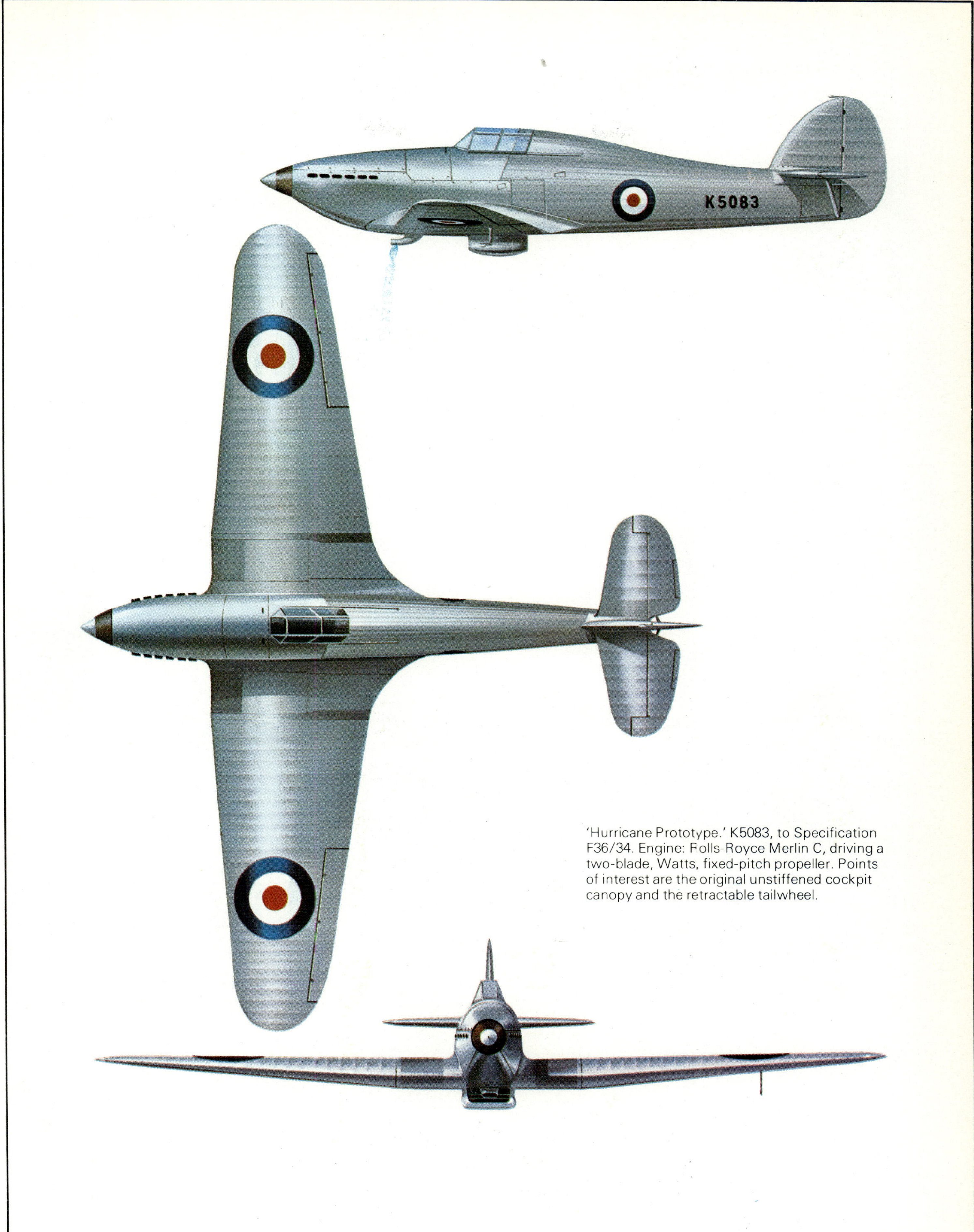

'Hurricane Prototype.' K5083, to Specification F36/34. Engine: Rolls-Royce Merlin C, driving a two-blade, Watts, fixed-pitch propeller. Points of interest are the original unstiffened cockpit canopy and the retractable tailwheel.

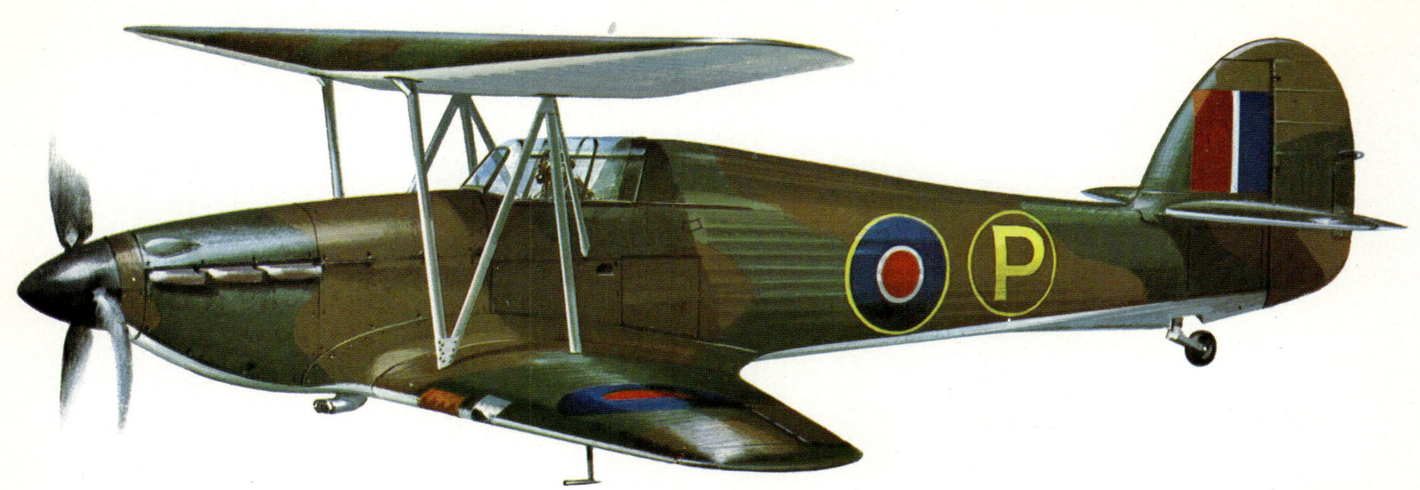

Above: 'Stol Hurricane.' Pre-dating the VTOL Harrier by twenty years was this Hillson FH40 slip-wing, or 'biplane' Hurricane. An old Hurricane MarkI (No L1884) was used for the experiment, the purpose of which was to provide extra lift to shorten the take-off run and so enable the fighter to take off from small airfields. After take-off, the wing was to be jettisoned. Several take-offs were made, but the top wing was never jettisoned in flight. The trials indicated that the idea was not practical, and the scheme was abandoned in 1943.

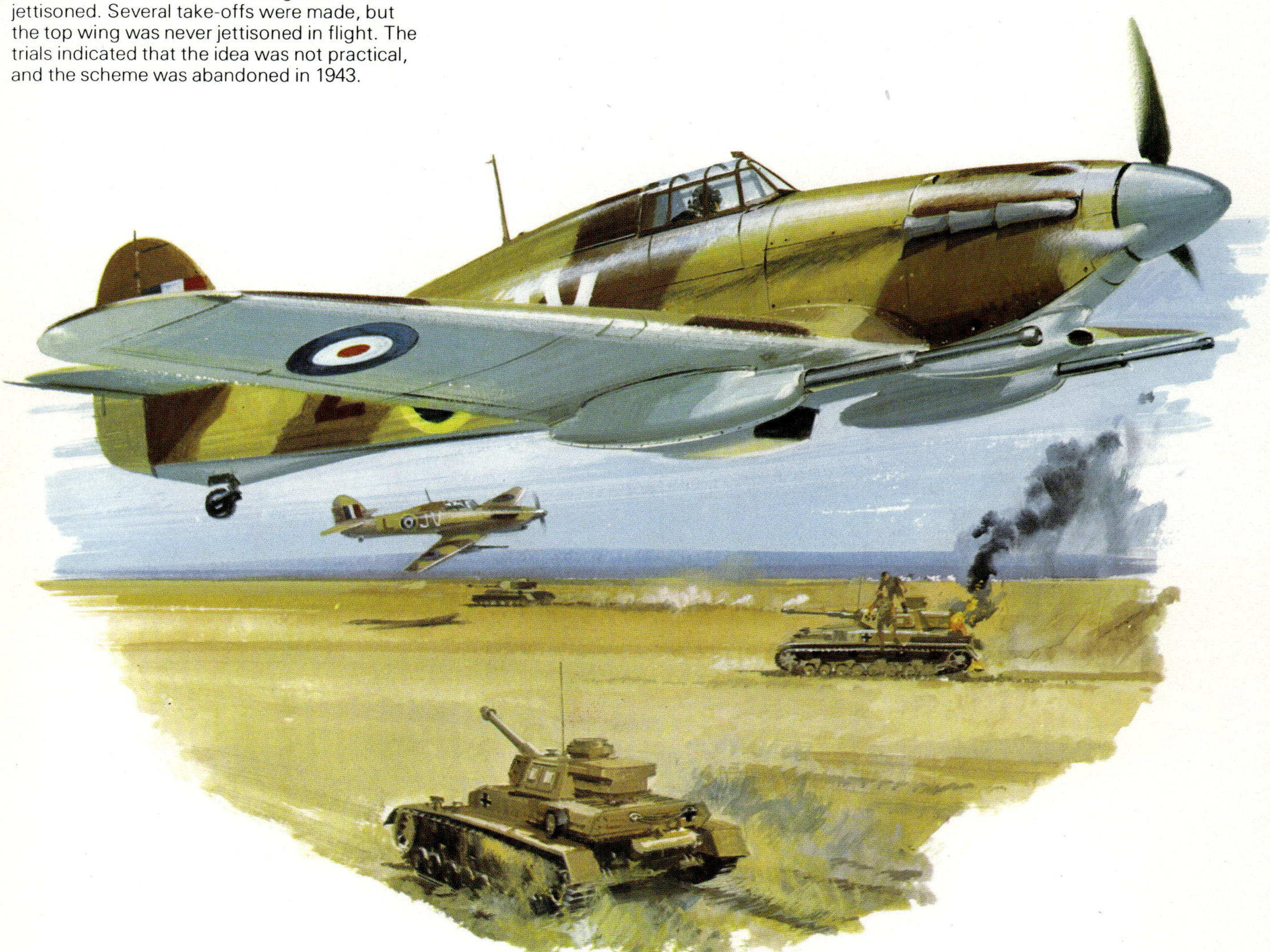

Above: 'Pick-a-Back Hurricane.' To overcome
Britain's lack of a long-range fighter, it was
proposed that bomber formations should tow
Hurricanes into action behind them, the
Hurricanes starting their engines and being
released if enemy fighters appeared. Another
idea was to carry them into battle on the backs
of Liberators as shown above, after the fashion
of the Short-Mayo Composite aircraft. Trials
indicated that prolonged towing caused the
engine to ice up so that it would not start. This
problem resulted in the abandoning of both the
towing scheme and the composite Liberator
plan.

Left: 'Can Opener.' Tank busting Hurricane IID,
armed with two 40mm cannon. These guns
were originally designed in 1939 for use as an
air-to-air weapon when it was considered that
one hit would be sufficient to guarantee the
destruction of an aircraft. This theory was
quickly dispelled when bombers survived
several hits from ground-based 40mm
anti-aircraft guns. The weapon was
subsequently developed as an anti-tank
weapon and mounted on the Hurricane
MarkIID. Up to four or five shots could be fired
in a typical pass, the guns being resighted
between each round due to the tendency for
the nose to drop when the guns fired. Hurricane
IIDs became the scourge of enemy tanks in the
Middle East and the Far East.

Below: 'Sunflower Seed.' One of the tactics
employed by the Luftwaffe against Allied
bomber formations over Europe was to fly
directly above a formation and then drop
bombs into it. One idea of countering this was
to equip the bombers with upward-firing
rockets, which would be released just before
the enemy aircraft got into position. To prove
the idea, a Hurricane was specially modified to
embody a single rocket tube, just aft of the
cockpit, as shown in the special drawing below.
On the first trial firing the fuselage was
damaged slightly, but the area around the
mouth of the tube was reinforced and other
fairings accomplished satisfactorily. It is
thought that the idea was subsequently used
operationally, but it was never adopted on a
large scale.

Above: 'Battle of Britain Hurricane.' Typical of the Hurricanes which fought in the Battle of Britain is L1592, illustrated above, powered by a 1,030hp Merlin III driving a three-blade de Havilland variable-pitch propeller, and armed with eight 0.303in Browning guns. This particular aircraft, in the markings of No 615 Squadron, Royal Auxiliary Air Force, is preserved in the Science Museum in London.

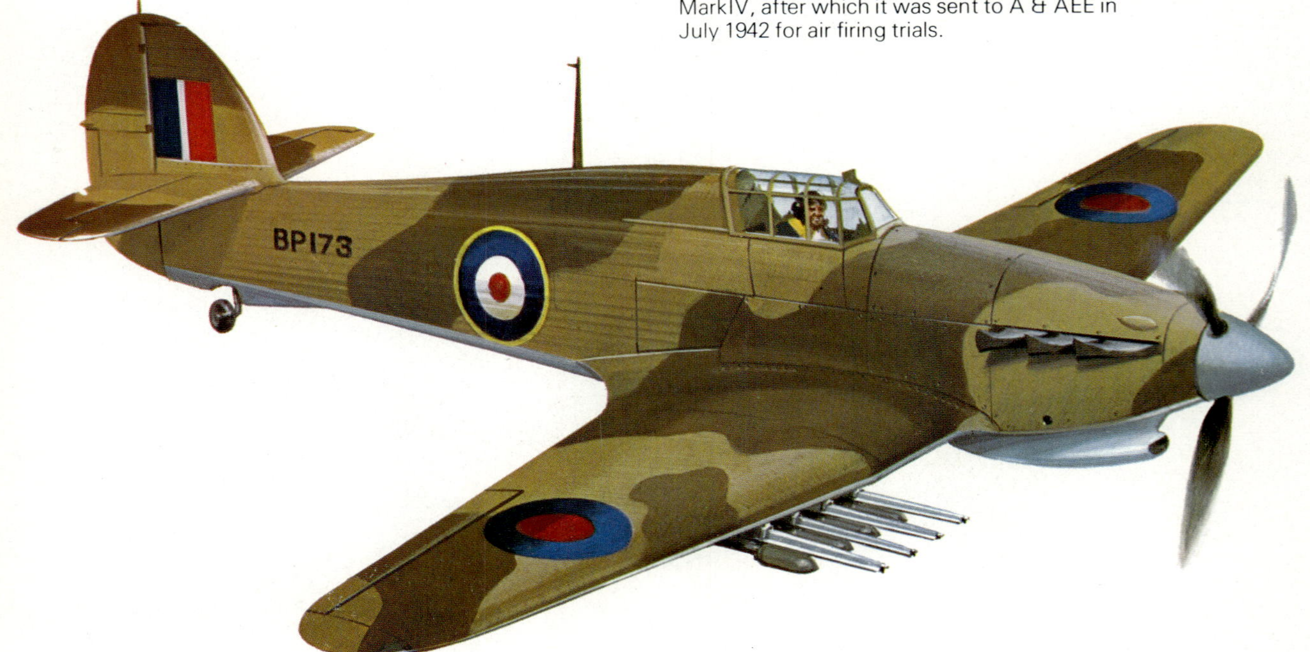

Below: 'Rocket-armed Hurricane IV.' Initially known as 'unrotating projectiles,' the rockets were crude, inaccurate, but highly destructive, a salvo being said to have the power of a broadside from a small cruiser. Hurricanes armed with rockets saw action in Europe, the Mediterranean theatre and in the Far East. They were also used extensively for attack on shipping. The aircraft illustrated, BP173, was built initially as a MarkIIB and delivered to No 47 MU, Sealand, in April 1942. It was then returned to Hawker Aircraft and modified into a MarkIV, after which it was sent to A & AEE in July 1942 for air firing trials.

Daily Express

No. 12,579 — Monday, September 16, 1940 — One Penny

R.A.F. smash Goering's Sunday raids on London by 400 planes

175 SHOT DOWN

Another bomb on Palace

5 RAIDERS CRASH ON LONDON

Fifth hospital bombed

SECOND WEEK OF THE BATTLE OF LONDON WAS OPENED BY GOERING WITH FOUR MORE BIG DAY AND NIGHT RAIDS—AND BY THE R.A.F. WITH A SMASHING VICTORY.

This morning it was learned that 175 enemy aircraft, out of 400 sent in many waves, were shot down in the three Sunday daylight raids on London. Thirty R.A.F. fighters were lost, but the pilots of ten are safe.

Again the Nazi murder bombers were sent against Buckingham Palace in a third deliberate attempt to kill the King and Queen. One bomb, which did not explode, damaged the Queen's private apartment.

Vengeance was swift. Almost immediately afterwards the plane which bombed the Palace was shot to pieces in mid-air by Spitfires.

Great air battles were fought out fiercely all the way from the coast to London as big formations of

Spitfires ambush raiders

SPITFIRES and Hurricanes, lying hidden in clouds, and

A NAZI bomber taking part in the Sunday raids on London is shot down in flames in the middle

A story that must earn a man the V.C.

St. Paul's saved:

1-ton bomb

A MONSTER bomb weighing fully a ton which for three days has been buried near St. Paul's Cathedral in London, exploded yesterday—but not at St. Paul's.

The courage and tenacity of a bomb disposal section under Lieu-

STOP PRESS

BERLIN RAID ALARM —GERMAN VERSION

BERLIN, Monday.—Air raid alarm sounded in Berlin at 11.28 p.m. yesterday, the all clear being given at 11.55 p.m. It was one of shortest Berlin has experienced. No planes were seen or heard over city and only evidence of the attack were two reports of anti-aircraft guns far away on the south-east.

German officials said: "This renewed attempt to bomb German civilians will be met by toward reprisals on London."

Officially stated, several British planes tried to reach Berlin. The statement added: "Well aimed anti-aircraft fire forced them to turn back before reaching defence barrage outside city.—B.U.P.

tenant R. Davies saved St. Paul's from being levelled to the ground. Instead, the bomb went off harmlessly on waste ground at Hackney Marshes

---

claimed: 100, actual 40; September 27th, claimed: 153, actual 55.

(2) The claims were published on the evening of the day they were made, so that although every effort was made at the pilot's interrogation to substantiate the claims, a complete check on figures was obviously not possible.

(3) In the heat of battle pilots were incapable of a cold dispassionate observation of events, concentrating as they had to on an aircraft in their gunsights or on their tails. Thus, it might happen that two pilots, unconscious of one another's presence, might attack the same aircraft, and afterwards, in all honesty, each claim an aircraft destroyed since both pilots had seen the enemy aircraft fall and crash. Finally, as is well known, aircraft are capable of surviving incredible damage, and undoubtedly many of the enemy aircraft, which to the Fighter Command pilots seemed doomed, managed somehow to return to their base.

Summing up—it was difficult, if not impossible, to arrive at an accurate total of enemy losses, however hard one tried. It is as simple as that.

In spite of the above, on no less than 24 days during the Battle of Britain, the number claimed was *less* than the number actually shot down. Overall, the accuracy of the claims was tolerable, amounting to some 65 per cent of the total actually destroyed. This percentage is much higher

A DAY TO REMEMBER

John Young, Night News Editor at the 'Daily Express' in 1940, vividly remembers the day of September 15th. It encompassed, he recalls, hours of the highest drama ever known in Fleet Street.

By early afternoon it had become evident that a crucial battle was being fought in the skies over South London, Kent, Surrey and Sussex. As the afternoon progressed, it was obvious the fighting was on a mammoth scale.

Reports came in steadily of aircraft shot down, both British and German. Hour by hour the totals mounted, and it became clear that the enemy had suffered a severe defeat. The details of the losses were obtained from official Air Ministry reports, and from staff reporters, local correspondents and agencies.

By the time darkness came and the battle had died down, it was calculated that the Germans had lost 175 aircraft. This total was submitted to the Ministry of Information for approval before it was published in the famous headline reproduced here. Later on, a recount increased the estimate of the number of German aircraft shot down to 185.

than achieved by the USAAF in its claims made of combat kills over Europe.

With reference to the fighting on September 15th, at that stage of the Battle the Germans genuinely thought that the Royal Air Force was virtually beaten, and they were shattered not only to see so many Hurricanes and Spitfires in the air, but also at the ferocity with which they pressed home their attacks. Luftwaffe pilots and their commanders were thoroughly shaken at the success of the British fighters in breaking up their bomber formations.

One German fighter pilot, who served in KG2, remarked to colleague Ted Hooton, author of *Spitfire Special*, that he well remembered the 15th. He and his fellow pilots were convinced that day if an RAF fighter could not shoot its opponent down, then it would ram it! This view was reinforced when a Hurricane hit a Do17 flying just in front of his aircraft. Later, the KG2 pilot himself was narrowly missed by a second Hurricane.

In retrospect, the significance of September 15th, 1940, is not so much the size of the claims or actual losses on one side or the other as the fact that Fighter Command knew that it had won a great victory, while the Luftwaffe realised that it had suffered a severe defeat.

Of the 328 bombers venturing over England that day, 51 were shot down or damaged beyond repair. This represents a loss rate of 12 per cent which is crippling.

It is little wonder then that in Germany, just after the Battle, the officer charged with keeping the official War Diary wrote: 'The enemy air force is still by no means defeated; on the contrary it shows increasing activity. . . The Fuhrer therefore decides to postpone Sea Lion (the code name for the invasion of Britain) indefinitely.'

Author's Diary Entry for September 15, 1940:

Air Raids.

1.	11.50 am-1.00 pm
2.	2.15 pm-3.20 pm
3.	7.15 pm-7.40 pm
4.	8.15 pm-8.15 am

Slept under the stairs. Terrific battle. 185 down. Bombs jettisoned 300 yards away.

SEPTEMBER 15, 1940 SCOREBOARD

During this day of crucial air battles over England, at least 30 of Fighter Command's 57 Squadrons are known to have been engaged in combat. These squadrons are listed below, together with their losses and the number of victories derived from individual pilot claims.

ROYAL AIR FORCE—FIGHTER COMMAND

	Squadron	Losses	Claims of Enemy Aircraft Shot Down
HURRICANES	No 46 Stapleford Tawney	Nil	5
	No 73 Debden/Castle Camps	1	3
	No 87 Exeter/South Cerney	Nil	1 (See Note)
	No 213 Tangmere	Nil	4
	No 229 Northolt	2	4½
	No 238 Middle Wallop	1	5
	No 242 Duxford/Coltishall	1	11½
	No 249 North Weald	Nil	7½
	No 253 Kenley	1	1
	No 257 Debden/Martlesham Heath	Nil	4½
	No 302 Leconfield	Nil	8
	No 303 Northolt	2	16
	No 310 Duxford	2	5½
	No 1 (RCAF) Northolt	2	3
	No 501 Kenley	2	6
	No 504 Hendon	3	7
	No 605 Croydon	2	9
	No 607 Tangmere	1	6½
	Hurricane Totals 18 Squadrons	20	108
SPITFIRES	No 19 Fowlmere	1	12½
	No 41 Rochford/Hornchurch	1	5½
	No 66 Gravesend	Nil	9
	No 72 Biggin Hill	Nil	6
	No 92 Biggin Hill	Nil	7½
	No 152 Warmwell	Nil	1
	No 222 Hornchurch/Rochford	Nil	1½
	No 266 Wittering	Nil	Nil
	No 602 Westhampnett	1	3
	No 603 Hornchurch	2	6
	No 609 Middle Wallop	1	6
	No 611 Fowlmere/Duxford	Nil	5
	Spitfire Totals 12 Squadrons	6	63
	GRAND TOTAL 30 SQUADRONS	26	171

Also given is a table of the true German losses as compiled from the Luftwaffe Quartermaster General records (6th Department) captured by the Allies at the end of the war. The total of 54 aircraft lost is the one now generally accepted by all leading air historians.

Squadrons which were not believed to be in action on September 15th are:

HURRICANE: No 1, Wittering; No 2, Castletown/Turnhouse; No 3, Acklington; No 43, Usworth; No 56, Boscombe Down; No 79, Pembrey, No 85, Church Fenton; No 111, Drem; No 145, Dyce/Montrose; No 151, Digby; No 232, Sumburgh; No 245, Aldergrove; No 263, Drem; No 306, Church Fenton; No 308, Squires Gate; No 312, Duxford; No 601, Exeter; No 615, Prestwick.

SPITFIRE: No 54, Catterick; No 64, Leconfield/Ringway; No 65, Turnhouse; No 74, Coltishall; No 234, St. Eval; No 610, Acklington; No 616, Kirton-in-Lindsey.

Note: The victory of No 87 Squadron should really be regarded separately from the main battle scoreboard, as this action was against a lone He111 weather flight reconnaissance over Bolt Head very early in the morning.

LUFTWAFFE LOSSES

Derived from the Luftwaffe Quartermaster General Records (6th Department) completed during the fortnight following the actions on September 15th.

Type of aircraft	Number lost totally over England, the Channel, France or unknown places (sea)	Number damaged
Bf109	22	2
Do17Z	20	10
He111	10	7
Ju88	2	2
TOTAL	54	21

Note: Two other Luftwaffe aircraft were lost on this day, one Do18 and one He59, but these losses were not due to the RAF.

AIR VICTORIES—CLAIMS

Prior to the changes introduced in August 1940, British and German methods of assessing air casualties were broadly similar, but the Luftwaffe was far less stringent in applying them.

Fighter Command instructions stated that for a confirmed loss, the enemy aircraft had to be seen on the ground or in the sea by a member of a crew or formation, or confirmed that it was destroyed from other sources, e.g. ships at sea or coastguards. The aircraft had to be seen to descend with flames issuing, and it was not sufficient if only smoke was seen. The aircraft must also be seen to break up in the air. For an unconfirmed loss, the enemy aircraft had to be seen to break off combat in circumstances which led our pilot to believe that it would be a loss. This method of assessment was used in the early part of the Battle of Britain, but in August, 1940 revised categories were applied which laid down that there were to be three categories of enemy casualties, destroyed, probably destroyed and damaged. The 'destroyed' category covered cases where the aircraft was clearly seen to hit the ground or the sea, where the aircraft was seen to break up in the air, or to descend in flames, whether or not confirmation from a second source was available. It also applied where the enemy aircraft was forced to descend and was captured, or when the pilot of a single-seater aircraft was seen to bale out.

The 'probably destroyed' category covered aircraft which were seen to break off combat in circumstances which led to the conclusion that it must be a loss although it was not actually seen to crash. The 'damaged' category covered cases in which the enemy aircraft was obviously considered damaged as a result of the attack of our aircraft, e.g. cases in which the undercarriage dropped off or engines or aircraft parts were shot away.

Giving the Hurricane Teeth

When the 'Private Venture Interceptor Monoplane,' from which the Hurricane evolved, was being developed in 1934, its armament consisted of two wing-mounted Browning machine-guns and two fuselage-mounted Vickers machine-guns. The Vickers guns were well proved and had been in service for many years. The Browning guns, on the other hand, were relatively new and thus somewhat of an unknown quantity.

Towards the end of 1933 the recently-formed Armament Research Division of the Air Ministry initiated an evaluation of various aircraft machine-guns. Samples of the Colt, Darne, Hispano, Kiraleji, Lewis, Madson, Spandau and Vickers were assessed in terms of reliability, rate of fire, and penetrative power. The study indicated that one gun was far superior to the others—the American Colt.

At this stage, however, this weapon fired U.S. 0.300in rifle-type rimless ammunition, and was thus unsuitable for use by the Royal Air Force. The Air Ministry contacted the U.S. manufacturers, the Colt Automatic Weapon Corporation, to ascertain whether or not the gun could be modified to accept British 0.303in rimmed ammunition without detriment to its reliability and very high rate of fire—about 1200 rounds per minute. The company replied that it could.

In 1934 it was becoming apparent that the increasing performance of aircraft, with the consequent reduction in aiming and firing times, was rendering the traditional four-gun armament inadequate. At an Air Ministry conference on July 19th, 1934, Capt F. W. Hill, Senior Ballistics Officer of the A. & A.E.E., Martlesham Heath, 'proved' that at least eight guns, each firing 1,000 rounds a minute, would be required to destroy a bomber in two seconds, this being the estimated time an aircraft would be held in sights.

In view of this, and as a result of the survey of weapons, the Air Ministry issued in 1934 a draft Specification F5/34 for a fighter, to be armed with either 6 or 8 forward-firing Colt-type machine guns. Such a heavy armament was then unprecedented, and the object of that part of the Specification was to initiate a study of the design problems of the performance penalties involved.

With the issue of this Specification, the Hawker design team began to consider ways of adapting their PV Interceptor Monoplane to meet the eight-gun requirement, at the same time continuing work on the 'basic' four-gun version.

The project became so promising that the Air Ministry drafted a Specification tailored to match the Hawker predictions. This was Specification F36/34, issued in September 1934. The armament specified was four

machine-guns, of a type to be determined later, with a firing time of not less than twenty seconds.

By January 1935, the Company had evolved a scheme whereby the eight guns called up in Specification F5/34 could be accommodated.

However, at this stage it was not known whether a licence could be obtained for manufacture of the Colt/Browning gun adapted for British 0.303in ammunition. Thus, the initial Air Ministry contract for the Hawker fighter issued in February 1935 was for one aircraft without any guns! Provision was, however, to be made for mounting two Vickers MkV guns in the fuselage and a Browning or Vickers gun in each wing. A licence for the Browning gun was ratified in July, 1935 and the contract was amended to call for two batteries of four Brownings located one in each wing and firing outside the propeller disc. As a standby, however, an alternative installation with Vickers guns was listed.

The decision to mount the guns in the wings had two interesting consequences. One, although the two Vickers guns were removed from the fuselage, this was not reduced in size. Thus the Hurricane was a little wider than was strictly necessary. Secondly, the request for the heavy eight-gun armament initiated a design study of metal stressed-skin wings in place of the original fabric-covered wings. Because of the extensive alterations required, however, the metal-skin wings did not appear on production aircraft until 1939.

Ballasted for eight Browning guns and ammunition, the Hurricane prototype first flew on November 6th, 1935. Guns were not installed until August, 1936. The Hurricane had got its teeth at last.

On Hurricane Is, produced in 1937, the lines of fire of the eight guns were arranged to converge at 650 yards, but this distance was progressively reduced to 200 yards. The

Above: Hurricane MarkIIC, armed with four 20mm cannon and equipped with jettisonable 44-gallon long-range fuel tanks, at Brooklands in 1942. The honour for utilising a modern 'drop-tank' installation appears to be shared equally between the Hurricane and the Japanese Zeke. The tanks slowed the Hurricane by some 30mph and also reduced its manoeuvrability. However, they assisted the Hurricane to become a most effective weapon against small German 'flak' ships and E-boats.

Above right: Hurricane MarkIICs of No 3 (Fighter) Squadron. These aircraft engaged in some of the early 'rhubarb' offensive sweeps over Northern France during 1941.

Centre right: Hurricane MarkI test-firing its eight 0.303in Browning machine-guns at the butts, somewhere in the Middle East. These guns gave a combined weight of fire of 10lb in a three-second burst. This compared with a weight of 18lb from a Bf109E, armed with two 7.9mm machine-guns and two 20mm cannon.

Right: Inboard gun bay showing four of the twelve 0.303in Browning guns forming the armament of the Hurricane MkIIB. These twelve guns had a weight of fire of 15lb in a three-second burst.

aircraft used for armament development was L1695. Armour-plate and a bullet-proof windscreen were added to production aircraft.

The exigencies of war necessitated the fitting of non-standard armament at times. For example, when during the Battle of Britain it was necessary to clear a small number of slightly damaged Hurricanes from the bombed premises of Rollasons, four aircraft were delivered for squadron service with only six guns.

During the Battle of Malta a number of Hurricane Is were also armed with only six guns, partly to conserve ammunition and partly reduce the take-off runs required on the bomb-scarred airfields in the summer heat.

Divergences from the 'standard' armament also included the four 0.50in. guns specified for the 80 Hurricanes planned for licensed-production at the Gosselies factory of Avions Fairey for the Belgian Air Force. However, only two of these had been completed by the time Belgium was invaded.

Although the standard eight-gun armament had proved devastating in battles ranging from Norway to the Middle East, and during the Battle of Britain, its effectiveness became reduced when the Germans started increasing armour protection on their aircraft. The need for some bigger teeth was becoming apparent.

Initial thoughts of a MarkII Hurricane, with increased armament, centred on fitting an additional four Browning guns, proposals for which Sydney Camm had submitted to the Air Ministry as early as January 1940. However, the heavy loss of Hurricanes in France in May, and the subsequent necessity to increase production; plus the fear of a shortage of Browning guns prevented the early adoption of the scheme. Thus the first 120 MarkIIs, powered by Merlin XXs were armed with just the normal eight guns. These aircraft designated MarkIIA, started entering service from the beginning of September 1940.

Following aircraft, with 12 guns, were designated IIBs. They were not popular with most pilots, partly due to the relative inaccuracy of the outer guns and partly because their extra weight located well out towards the wing tips,

Far left top: Re-arming the four 20mm Hispano cannon of a Hurricane MarkIIC. Both drum-feed and chatellerault belt ammunition feeds were utilised. Weight of fire of a three-second burst, 35lb. Drawings on the side of the cockpit, just visible on the original photograph, indicate that this particular machine had already destroyed three railway locomotives and one enemy aircraft.

Above: 'Anti-tank Hurricane.' One of the most significant armament developments of the Hurricane was the installation of two 40mm anti-tank guns. Two 0.303in machine-guns were also fitted which fired alternate ball and tracer ammunition and were used for sighting the cannon. These anti-tank Hurricanes were first used in the Western Desert in 1942 during the Battle of Bir Hakim. In the first month of operations in the Western Desert the six MarkIIDs attached to No 6 Squadron destroyed 26 tanks, 31 troop carriers, plus innumerable lorries, petrol bowsers and guns.

Above centre: Prototype 40mm gun installation under development in the Hawker Experimental Department at Kingston. In addition to the Vickers Type S gun installation, Hawkers also designed an installation for Rolls-Royce BF (belt-feed) 40mm guns.

Left: Most production MarkIIDs were fitted with Vickers guns, which carried 15 rounds per gun in a drum, compared with the 12 belt-fed rounds on the Rolls-Royce guns. The armour protection on the tank-busting Hurricanes was increased by 368lb giving the aircraft an all-up weight of 8,218lb.

significantly reduced the rate of roll, already less than that of the Bf109.

Schemes for a cannon-armed Hurricane were considered as early as late 1935. However, at that time only the fabric-winged prototype, with its two-blade propeller existed, and it was estimated that the installation of four of these heavy weapons—they weighed about a hundredweight—would reduce the speed from about 315mph to 270mph. This was obviously too low for a modern interceptor and the idea was shelved.

In the Spring of 1939 two 20mm Oerlikons were installed under the wings of Hurricane L1750 for air firing trials. This installation was associated with the development of the Westland Whirlwind, and little immediate thought was given to fitting such armament to production Hurricanes.

Thus, it was not until May 1940, that serious proposals were made for installing cannon in the Hurricane. Rather surprisingly, little official support was offered, so Hawkers 'p.v.'d' a trial installation of four cannon in a pair of damaged wings which were subsequently fitted to a Mark I fuselage and flown. The air firing trials conducted in August were so encouraging that the aircraft was allocated to No 151 (Fighter) Squadron at North Weald so that operational experience could be gained during the Battle of Britain. It is not known, however, whether the aircraft did ever see action, or what pilots thought of the heavily-armed fighter.

Production cannon-armed Hurricanes, designated MarkIICs started coming off the production lines in May 1941 and entered service about a month later.

These aircraft, when fitted with long-range fuel tanks, proved ideal for the great fighter 'rhubarb' sweeps made over Northern France during 1941, when great quantities of enemy shipping and road and rail transport were shot up. Hurricane MarkIICs, of which 4,711 were built in Britain, also fought as day and night fighters and engaged in intruder, reconnaissance, air/sea rescue and many other duties.

Left: A Hurricane MarkIID attacking a German tank in the Western Desert. One drawback of the installation was that each shot caused the nose to drop by about 5°, which meant that the target had to be resighted between rounds.

Below: Hurricane IV, with two 40mm Vickers anti-tank guns. Most of these Marks of aircraft were powered by the more powerful 1,620bhp Merlin 27s, although a few had Merlin 24s rated to give the same power. This Mark of Hurricane was developed especially for ground attack or close-support duties in North Africa. It had a 'universal' wing capable of carrying any external store, but with an internal armament of only two Browning machine-guns.

Big Teeth Hurricanes

ROCKET HURRICANES. To increase their noise while diving towards their target and so further demoralise the enemy, Junkers Ju87Bs were reported to have been fitted with wind-operated sirens. No such devices were necessary to increase the terror of rocket-armed Hurricanes. The rockets, initially known as 'UPs,' standing for 'Unrotating Projectiles' were quite crude weapons. They consisted simply of a 40-pound cast-iron warhead attached to a length of three-inch iron pipe containing the propellant, with three flat plates comprising the tail fins. Later, the weight of the warhead was increased to 60lb. In action, however, the rockets were deadly, although rather inaccurate. Considered to have the destructive power of a broadside from a naval destroyer, they caused great havoc and destruction among enemy armoured vehicles during the last two years of the war. One week before VE-day, 25 enemy ships in the Gulf of Trieste surrendered to rocket-firing Hurricanes of No 6 Squadron.

BOMBER HURRICANES. Although the concept of fighters carrying bombs dates back to the SE5a of the 1914-18 war which used 20lb Cooper bombs for ground strafing attacks, it was the Hurricane which brought the fighter bomber into prominence as a really useful weapon of modern war. It was the proponent of the tactical support aircraft of today.

'Hurri-bombers' proved effective in all theatres of the war, but probably reached their zenith in 1943 during the closing stages of the North African campaign. With the enemy compressed into the Cape Bon area of Tunisia, No 241 Squadron alone made over 180 sorties in a single day. The enthusiasm for the task of striking the enemy as hard as possible built up to the extent that, to save time, ground crews met returning aircraft at the end of the runway. This resulted in Hurricanes being serviced, refuelled, rearmed and turned round for take-off in eight minutes.

Above right: Hurricane MkIV armed with eight 60lb rockets. This aircraft was originally built as a MkIIB and delivered to No 47 Maintenance Unit, Sealand in April, 1942. It was returned to Hawkers and modified into a MkIV and then sent to A & AEE in July for trials.

Top far right: Re-arming a rocket Hurricane.

Right: Hurri-bomber carrying two 500lb bombs. This aircraft, BE492, was one of a formation of nine machines which, on May 15th 1942, attacked and sank three E-boats in the English Channel.

Centre far right: Hurricane Z3451, a MarkIIA, at Boscombe Down in March 1942, fitted with SBCs — Small Bomb Containers — under the wings. The SBCs could accommodate a number of fragmentation bombs, training bombs, or two Smoke Curtain Installations — SCIs. This type of store was used during several of the 'secret agent' type of operations carried out over Europe during 1943 and 1944.

Bottom far right: Bombing up a Hurricane MarkIIB of No 175 (Fighter) Squadron, based at Warmwell, on the South coast of England. Of interest is the shield on the side of the fuselage. These were installed on all Hurricanes destined for night-flying duties — and many others — and protected the pilot from the glare of the exhaust flames which could otherwise temporarily destroy his night vision.

Hurricanes for £50

Most of the 14,000 Hurricanes built were generally reckoned to have cost about £5,000 each, although the true figure is undoubtedly higher than this.

However, several hundred Hurricanes were produced for £50 each. These were the special 'decoy' Hurricanes manufactured in 1940.

The feasibility of dummy aircraft, and dummy airfields, had been studied by the Air Ministry as early as 1938. The idea was considered worth following up by Bomber Command and Coastal Command, but the C-in-C Fighter Command indicated that, if there was any money to spare, he would prefer it to be spent on real fighters!

However, the idea gathered momentum and by the middle of 1939 plans were in hand for a number of dummy airfields, to be located east of a line from Perth, in the North, through Birmingham to Southampton on the South coast. These decoys were not intended to represent major bases, but rather the 'satellite' airfields earmarked for use in time of war. The idea was that each would display up to 10 dummy aircraft, plus the vehicles, buildings and dummy flare paths and landing lights necessary for realism. They were to be manned by men based at the adjacent parent station, who upon receipt of an air raid, would take up their position and by switches operate the dummy lights in accordance with a carefully planned sequence to give the impression of an airfield at work.

Plans and Specification 23/38 were drawn up for three dummy aircraft—for Fairey Battles and Armstrong Whitworth Whitleys, in addition to the Hurricanes. To help produce these dummy aircraft the Air Ministry considered enlisting the aid of the film industry in Britain because it was 'accustomed to deception of all kinds.'

The Specification for the 'target' Hurricanes, the term by which the decoy aircraft were known, laid down that the dummy aircraft must be identical in size and outline to their real counterpart, and stated that any shadow cast on the ground should be undetectable from the real thing, to foil skilled interpreters of reconnaissance photographs. They also had to be reasonably resistant to weather and be capable of folding flat for easy transport. Almost above all they had to be cheap—no more than £50 each.

The dummy or 'target' Hurricanes were made by Green Brothers, at Hailsham in Sussex, who had a reputation for making good-quality folding furniture. The Company was requested by the Air Ministry to produce a target Hurricane in September, 1940. Although the Specification stressed the importance of realism, all the Ministry gave the Company was a small postcard size photograph, without any measurements. Eventually— after a great deal of argument—the Ministry relented and full-size details were supplied.

Early experiments showed that the dummies could be mounted on trestles, without undercarriage legs and

still escape detection. If an enemy pilot flew low enough to spot the absence of an undercarriage he was obviously low enough to spot the dummy.

The Green Brothers' target Hurricanes were made with wooden formers to give the general shape, to which were fixed wooden 'stringers,' over which canvas was stretched and painted. The fuselage was made in two parts, and to it was assembled the wings, tailplane, and the fin and rudder. The completed dummy was mounted on a light metal stand with wheels, so that it could be easily pushed into position and to enable it to be moved around as required.

The first decoy airfield for Hurricanes was completed near Wittering in September, 1939. It was so realistic that the problem arose of how to prevent pilots flying the real things from attempting to land on it. Several ideas were considered, the final solution being a red Aldis lamp, which was flashed from the site by an airman if an aeroplane appeared to be making a landing.

To increase the realism, most of the decoy airfields on which Hurricane dummies were deployed were fitted with dummy night flare paths and approach lighting, as installed on Q-sites.

Dummies were deployed not only on decoy airfields, for it was realised that they could also serve a useful purpose if they were used on operational airfields, to cover up for real aircraft moved to another base or, merely distributed among the real aircraft, to increase their apparent strength.

By the Autumn of 1940 three Bomber Groups and five Fighter Groups had each been allocated a 'station' complement of dummies. Thus, overnight, the strength of the Royal Air Force was reinforced dramatically by 168 'Wellingtons,' and 240 'Hurricanes,' 'Spitfires' and 'Defiants.' Passable 'Defiants,' it was discovered, could be made by only minor modifications to Spitfire dummies.

Altogether Green Brothers made about 500 of the £50 Hurricanes. They served their purpose well, for the Company was kept busy sending replacements and patching up bullet holes.

The K-sites and Q-sites as a whole were highly successful. By the middle of 1940 the Luftwaffe had carried out raids on Donna Nook for Northcoates; on Folkingham for Grantham; Lakenheath for Feltwell; and Coxford Heath for Bircham Newton. A year later real Royal Air Force stations had been attacked 304 times, while in the same period decoy airfields had been attacked 322 times!

These decoy airfields—and the special £50 Hurricanes—played a valuable part in diverting enemy activities, and undoubtedly saved many operational aircraft from destruction, diverted much damage away from their parent stations and, above all, saved many lives.

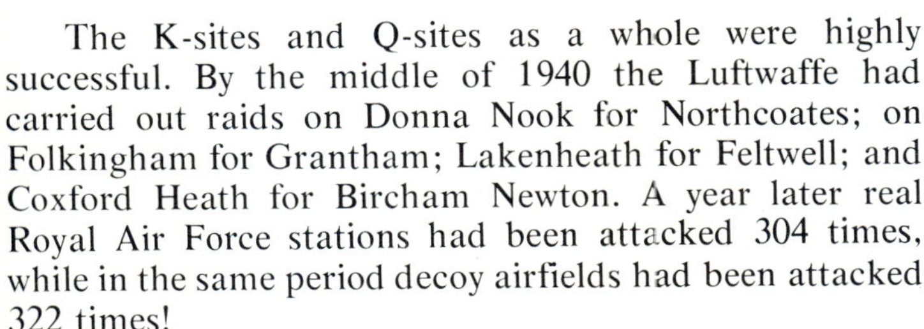

LOCATION OF TARGET HURRICANE K-SITE DECOY AIRFIELDS IN BRITAIN

Airfield	Location of Decoy
Acklington	*Longhoughton
Church Fenton	*Menthorpe
Wittering	Alwalton
Duxford	*Horseheath
Northolt	*Barnet
North Weald	*Nazeing
Hornchurch	*Bulphan
Biggin Hill	*Lullingstone
Tangmere	*Gumber

*Indicates decoy airfield also equipped with Q-site dummy flarepath and lighting.

DECOY HURRICANES ABROAD

In addition to the decoy Hurricanes produced in Britain, many others were made abroad to deceive the enemy in other lands. The pictures here show some such Hurricanes being produced from 'local resources' in Cyprus.

Hurricanes at War

Right: 'In France.' March 1940. No 87(F) Squadron. This was one of four (Nos 85, 87, 607 and 615) Hurricane squadrons forming the Air Component deployed in France, after the outbreak of war, to provide fighter cover for the British Expeditionary Force. Other Hurricane squadrons, Nos 1 and 73, protected the offensive force known as the Advanced Air Striking Force. The French airfields lacked proper drainage and the muddy surfaces provided a severe test for the rugged undercarriage on the Hurricane. In the bitter fighting preceding the fall of France the Air Component lost 195 Hurricanes and the AASF 66.

Below: 'In Iceland.' 1941. Hurricane MarkIIAs of No 1423 Flight, formerly part of No 98 (Bomber) Squadron. Judging from the rubble in the foreground even the Hurricane's undercarriage, sturdy as it was, would have a hard time surviving a swing off the paved runway.

Below right: 'Somewhere in England.' Hurricane simulates a 'hostile' aircraft shooting up an HQ during a simulated attack put on for the benefit of war correspondents visiting a coastal artillery regiment.

Top: 'With the WAAF.' Sea Hurricane IA being woman-handled into position at a shore station at which training was undertaken for duties on the merchant aircraft carriers then coming into service.

Above: 'At Sea.' Sea Hurricane landing on a carrier. Hurricanes not only fought from carriers, they were often transported in them. In March 1942, two squadrons, Nos 30 and 273, were transported from Egypt to Ceylon in the carrier 'Indomitable.' The aircraft were stored in the hangars without wings in order to squeeze them all in. When the carrier approached within flying distance of the destination, the Hurricanes were assembled and flown off. Lacking proper equipment, the assembly involved lifting the wings manually and holding them in position until they were secured. One can imagine what this task was like, below decks in the tropics.
One Hurricane, after taking off, reported a glycol leak and had to return to the carrier, the pilot making a breath-holding superb landing. On disembarking at Trincomalee, this Hurricane was dismantled and put on a train to catch its colleagues at Colombo. Unfortunately, during the journey, sparks from the wood-fired engine blew back and set the craft alight.

In the Desert

COMBAT REPORT

In November 1941, having recently converted to Hurricanes from Lysanders, the pilots of No 208 Squadron were not particularly practised in modern fighter tactics. This did not prevent them from making good use of the excellent flying qualities of the Hurricane, as is indicated by this official recommendation for the award of the Distinguished Flying Cross to Flying Officer Cotton.

'At 1530 hours on November 29th 1941 Flying Officer P. T. Cotton took off from LG134 to carry out a tactical reconnaissance in the Acroma-Tobruk-El Adem area. He was unescorted. Flying Officer Cotton had completed most of his task and was flying from El Adem to El Gubbi when he noticed two fighter aircraft. Thinking they were Me109s he immediately pulled the emergency boost out and opened up, at the same time losing height and weaving to keep the two aircraft in view. The Me109s closed to 300 yards on the starboard beam and commenced their attack. One broke away and started a stern attack, whereupon Flying Officer Cotton flicked his aircraft over in a violent right hand turn and spiralled towards the earth. At ground level he made for home on a southeast course but found the 109s again on him. They attacked him individually from astern, the quarter, and once from head on. Each successive attack was foiled by Flying Officer Cotton's evasive tactics which were to complete a 360° turn, very tight and fast, each time making a little headway southeast. The chase and the attacks went on for nearly half an hour during which time Cotton's aircraft was repeatedly hit. He managed to get in several bursts at the enemy aircraft but apparently without success. Finally the 109s exhaused their ammunition and broke off the assault. Flying Officer Cotton's aircraft was feeling the strain, and the engine already spluttering and faltering, gave out and he forced landed only six miles from LG134 causing little damage to the aircraft. He was able to get his valuable information back to 30 Corps Headquarters.'

Above left: The desert was their kingdom. An unusual view of Hurricanes taking off somewhere in the Western Desert in 1941. The need for 'tropical' filters is apparent. In the desert operations the Hurricane gained most of its laurels through its army-supporting roles rather than its achievements as an interceptor. Its presence in the area was inaugurated by a solitary machine which had been flown to Khartoum in 1939 for trials with a tropical filter. Although unarmed, the Hurricane was flown up to the front line where it made several sorties daily from different landing grounds in an attempt to make the Italians believe that Britain had a strong force of modern monoplane fighters in the area!

Above: Gloster-built tropical Hurricane MarkI with the rare black/white under-wing colour schemes. Some pilots have 'sworn' that such aircraft never operated in the Middle East, but this photograph seems to provide evidence otherwise.

Left: Pilots, in somewhat unusual head gear, at Takoradi. This port, on the Gold Coast, was selected in 1940 as the base to which Hurricanes would be shipped by sea from England, and then uncrated, assembled and flown to the desert war zones. The air journey, of up to 4,000 miles, involved long and fatiguing stages, along which the Hurricanes were navigated by a Blenheim or other larger multi-crew aircraft. By the middle of 1943, over 5,300 American and British aircraft, including fighters, bombers and transports had followed the by then well-established route.

The MacRobert Fighters

Comprising nine Gladiators and four Hurricanes, No 94 Squadron was sent to Habbaniyah, Iraq, in May, 1941 following the seizure of power of the pro-Axis Rashid Ali, where the Hawker fighters carried out strafing attacks against Iraqi motor transport on the Baghdad-Falluja road. However, they had insufficient range to reach the bases from which the German aircraft were operating, and so two further machines, equipped with fixed 44-gallon long-range fuel tanks, were sent from Aboukir.

Flown by Flt Lt Sir Roderic A. MacRobert and Fg Off J. G. Sandison, these new aircraft destroyed a number of Heinkel He111s and Messerschmitt Bf110s over Mosul and Erbil. Then MacRobert was shot down and killed. Sir Roderic was the third and last of three brothers to lose his life in the war. To commemorate their memory, Lady MacRobert donated three Hurricane MarkIICs to the Middle East Air Command, each bearing the family crest and the name of one of her sons.

Left: Sir Roderic.

Right: Sir Ian.

Below left: Sir Alasdair.

Below: Photograph of Hurricane Sir Alasdair autographed for the author in 1942.

Below right: Air Marshal McClaughry shaking hands with Plt Off A. Walker, pilot of the Hurricane commemorating Sir Roderic.

In the Far East

When the Hurricane first came up against the Japanese Zero fighter in the Far East, it was found to possess a marginal edge in speed, climb and manoeuvrability over the redoubtable Japanese fighter above 20,000ft. Unfortunately, the Japanese pilots tended to operate well below this altitude, with the result the Zero outclassed the Hurricane by a wide margin.

The Hurricane fared better against other Japanese aircraft particularly the fighters and bombers operating with the Japanese Army Air Force, and it excelled in ground attack duties, both during the initial rapid retreats in that war zone and during the slow process of re-conquest.

Hurricanes bore the major share of air defence and tactical support during the years from 1942 to 1944, when they were joined by Spitfires and Thunderbolts. For its part in helping to hold Imphal, the vital gateway to India, the Hurricane was mentioned in an official Despatch thus: 'The enemy's efforts to deploy in the Imphal plain during May 1944, were decisively defeated by Hurricane attacks at short intervals on any concentrations reported by ground troops through our Army Support Control, operating at a high standard of efficiency.'

Left: On the road to Mandalay. The Aya Bridge over the Irrawaddy dwarfs a low-flying Hurricane IV reconnaissance fighter.

Below left: Presenting a good straffing target for enemy fighters, a line of Hurricanes are serviced before taking off from an airfield in India.

Below: Hurricane IIC night fighters on an evening patrol.

TANKS A MILLION. The four 20mm cannon armament of the Hurricane MarkIIC proved particularly effective against Japanese infantry positions, vehicles and light armour. One particularly memorable operation took place in February, 1945 near Myinmu during the final Allied offensive. It was in this area the Japanese had concentrated a strong force of precious tanks. To camouflage these, each had cunningly been encased in what appeared to be a small native hut of wood and straw. One Hurricane pilot, suspicious, fired at one 'hut,' blew the roof off, to reveal its tank. He summoned help from other Hurricanes and soon 12 tanks had been put out of action. A nearby British infantry division radioed the following signal: 'Nippon Hardware Corporation has gone bust. Tanks a million.'

Left: Hurricane MarkIIC fighter bomber has its 20mm cannon serviced during a 40 hour inspection on an airfield in Burma.

Above: Hurricane MarkIIIC being serviced on a forward airstrip in Burma.

RETRIEVING A CRASHED HURRICANE

Above right: Using a 'wrecker' crane, members of the Royal Air Force Salvage Unit lift the nose of a crashed Hurricane 'somewhere in Burma' so that the undercarriage can be lowered to assist dismantling which is already under way.
In the foreground, a Bren gun team lie ready should the Japanese try and take their prize from them.

Right: On this occasion the operation is successful and the Hurricane, now dismantled and on lorries, passes through an abandoned village on its way back to the repair unit. In the jungle, improvisation was the order of the day. Hurricanes which had lost their tailwheels were fitted with bamboo tailskids; one Hurricane even flew into combat fitted with an entire longeron made from bamboo.

Hurricanes at Sea

One of the by-products of the German occupation of Norway and France was command of the entire north European seaboard. This was used to good effect, and British shipping losses increased alarmingly. Many of the losses were due to attacks by the Focke-Wulf Fw200C Condor long-range reconnaissance bombers which often flew long sorties, starting from northern Norway, flying well out into the Atlantic around Ireland, finally landing near Bordeaux.

The ideal answer to this menace would have been to escort convoys with carriers, but Britain had lost the *Courageous* and *Glorious* early in the war and their replacements could not be accelerated. Many antidotes were studied, one of which was the idea of mounting Hurricanes on catapults fitted to the bows of merchant ships. The idea was that two or more such ships, loaded with their normal cargo as well as a Hurricane, would accompany each convoy. When an enemy aircraft was sighted, a Hurricane would be launched to intercept. After combat the Hurricane would either ditch in the sea or try to reach the nearest land. Winston Churchill was impressed—some say he conceived the idea—and gave his blessing to the project.

However, as is often the case, having the idea was the easy part; putting the idea into practice was quite another matter and brought forward Britain's aptitude for improvisation when under duress. Hydraulically-operated catapults were normally used to launch aircraft from ships, but these were pieces of precision equipment, far too heavy, complicated and expensive for use on merchantmen. Thus the idea of using rocket catapults was born, the supply of 3in rockets then being plentiful.

Initial trials were conducted on ground-based rocket catapults at Farnborough. A rocket launch was an awe-inspiring event when seen for the first time. As described by one eyewitness, it was 'a vast noise, accompanied by sheets of flame and loud explosions long after the aircraft had been launched.'

With the problem of the catapults solved, 35 ships, ranging from 2,500 to 12,000 tons, were modified. With a catapult fitted the vessels were officially known as CAM-ships—Catapult Armed Merchantmen.

On the aircraft side, Hawkers were asked in October, 1940, if it was possible to fit catapult spools to a Hurricane. Hawkers replied 'yes,' stating that a prototype could be ready in five weeks. Incredibly, in spite of the seriousness of the situation, it was not until the middle of January that a 'go-ahead' was received. Initially 20 sets of catapult spools were ordered, an additional 30 being requested shortly afterwards.

Aircraft fitted with the spools were known as Sea Hurricane MarkIAs. Catapult development and training was carried out at Speke near Liverpool. In contrast to the comments of ground staff, pilots not only considered the

Left: Hurricane being mounted on the catapult fitted to the bow of a CAM-ship. On this wartime photo the aircraft serial number has been erased by the censor. It is, in fact, V6756, a Hurricane 1, originally built by the Gloster Aircraft Co in 1940, and converted to a Sea Hurricane Mark 1A.
Many of the Sea Hurricanes, in fact, were veterans of the Battle of Britain, which had been repaired and converted after suffering damage due to enemy action.

Below: Loading the 'catafighters,' as the Sea Hurricane 1As were popularly known, presented problems, particularly at distant ports with limited facilities. In this picture many hands make relatively easy the task of pushing a Hurricane on to a lighter, believed to be at Gibraltar.

Bottom: A lighter, loaded with two 'catafighters,' on its way to a CAM-ship.

Below left: Hoisting a catafighter from its lighter. Notice in this wartime print that the censor has deleted shipping in the background. The organisation of the CAM-ships, known as the Merchant Service Fighter Unit, soon grew from a few Battle of Britain volunteer pilots into a highly specialised independent fighting unit with pools of Hurricanes and pilots in Canada and Russia.

noise less harsh, but the acceleration smoother, than that of a normal hydraulic-catapult launch.

For a catapult-launching, the flaps were set for takeoff and the engine run at full throttle. The pilot pressed his head back against the head-pad to protect his neck, and then held up one hand to indicate he was ready. The firing of the catapult accelerated the Hurricane to a speed of 75mph in a run of 70ft, at the end of which the catapult was arrested by an hydraulic buffer and the aircraft continued on its flight.

The first CAM-ship to go to sea was the SS *Michael E.* on May 27th, 1941, but it was torpedoed and sunk together with its Hurricane. Shortly afterwards the first Sea Hurricane was launched 'in anger' from a CAM-ship, but no enemy aircraft was destroyed.

CAM-ship duties were most arduous, for whatever the outcome of any ensuing combat, the pilot was faced with a difficult choice: whether to try and reach land—not easy as the normally great distance involved imposed navigational problems—or to ditch near the convoy and hope to be picked up.

However, the Hurricane was not a pleasant aircraft to ditch in the sea. The large belly radiator acted as a bucket and dragged the nose in so that the craft often sank in seconds.

For this reason, if pilots could not reach land, they often preferred to bale out. The suggested technique for this operation was to: 'open the canopy, roll upside down and push the stick forward.' One was then shot out of the cockpit like the proverbial cork from a champagne bottle.

At best though this meant parachuting into water that was often rough and always icy. Landing near a ship did not guarantee being picked up because, not only were a pilot and his raft difficult to sight, if the presence of enemy U-boats was suspected, the ships could not afford the risk of stopping.

To reduce the wastage of aircraft it was suggested that the undercarriage should be removed and the empty wheel bays filled with additional fuel to give an increased range and allow the pilot to reach land from greater distances. However, this would have meant certainly damaging an aircraft every time a landing was made. With the undercarriage on, normal landings could sometimes be made at shore bases.

Eventually, in the autumn of 1941, 44-gallon drop tanks were fitted under the wings of the Sea Hurricanes. These enabled pilots to reach land from much greater distances from land and raised morale. On the debit side, the tanks reduced the Hurricane's manoeuvrability and also necessitated an increase in catapult power.

Although thus equipped a CAM-ship was a threat to potential raiders, the ship itself was defenceless against air attack. Guns were out of the question; these being too heavy for the average merchantship and not available in sufficient quantities anyway.

To provide some protection certain CAM-ships were thus fitted with an improvised anti-aircraft weapon of fiendish ingenuity although the protection provided was more psychological than practical. The weapon consisted of a length of 3in piping mounted vertically, into the

bottom end of which could be fed steam from the high pressure turbines. If an enemy aircraft was sighted, a Mills bomb, with the pin removed, was dropped down the tube, the sides of which held the arming lever in the safe position. At the appropriate moment, the cock was opened, admitting steam to the bottom of the tube. The grenade was expelled upwards with great velocity to explode—with luck—in front of the attacking aircraft!

By the end of 1941 CAM-ship Hurricanes had shot down about six of the long-range German raiders over the Atlantic. This rate of loss was not severe enough to cause the Condors to cease their attacks entirely, but they lessened appreciably when the CAM-ships went into operation. Losses of shipping due to this form of attack reduced to negligible proportions. However, their relative inflexibility and the problem of provisioning replacement Hurricanes at distant ports of call, brought about their end quite quickly. Their task was taken over by Hurricanes on MAC-ships—Merchant Aircraft Carriers. These were mini-carriers, comprising merchant ships with their superstructure removed, an offset bridge added and a simple flight deck accommodating up to six Sea Hurricanes and, sometimes, a similar number of Swordfish torpedo bombers. The MAC-ship Hurricanes, equipped with an arrester hook as well as catapult spools, were known as Sea Hurricanes Mark IBs.

Plans were also prepared for folding the wings of the Hurricane, but these were never put into production.

Far left: Artist's impression of the CAM-ship 'Maplin' in heavy seas. Formerly the Fyffe ship SS 'Erin,' she was selected because her relatively high cruising speed, 16 knots, essential for delivering her pre-war loads of bananas before they rotted, gave a useful speed increment when turned into wind before launching the Hurricane.

This particular ship was one of the few, if not the only CAM-ship, to carry two Sea Hurricanes. The second one was stowed on deck with inches to spare, between the mast and the bridge, where it was protected only by a tarpaulin. When the first Hurricane had been launched, the second one was swung round the mast, using the ship's normal steam-operated derricks, on to the catapult. As the aft derrick could only pivot 90 degrees, the manoeuvre entailed transferring the aircraft to the forward derrick, to get it into position. The difficulty of doing this and of lowering the aircraft on to the catapult trolley with the ship pitching and rolling can be imagined. The artist recalls that to hold it steady required the efforts of every 'cook and stoker' on board.

Of interest to the pedantic is that the 'Maplin' was not truly a merchant ship, except in origin. Properly titled HMS 'Maplin,' she was a Royal Naval vessel, crewed by the Navy for her specific role. No 804 Fleet Air Arm Squadron manned the aircraft, unlike the 'ordinary' CAM-ships on which RAF personnel flew the Hurricanes. Two other Hurricane-armed vessels were operated by the Royal Navy.

Normal CAM-ships stayed with their convoy for the complete voyage. HMS 'Maplin,' sailing from Britain, escorted its convoy as far as Iceland and then turned back to escort another one on its way to Britain. / Drawing by John Scott.

Above: Sea Hurricane Mark 1Bs ranged on the deck of HMS 'Furious' escorting a convoy to Malta. In addition to duties in the Mediterranean, Sea Hurricane 1Bs achieved great successes during 1942 in convoys to Murmansk, which were invariably subjected to heavy attacks by bombers based in Norway and Finland. During one particularly fierce attack forty bombers were shot down for the loss of four Sea Hurricanes.

Left: Artist's impression of the end of a Condor. The story starts with a Condor being spotted circling the convoy at a distance of some 15 miles. The Hurricane, on the CAM-ship 'Maplin,' was not launched because the Condor did not attack. The Condor then flew off in a southerly direction. It had scarcely disappeared from sight when a second Condor appeared, at sea level, approaching the convoy fast. The Hurricane was launched immediately, but before it could turn, the Condor had dropped a stick of bombs across a ship, setting the bridge on fire. Seconds later a shell hit the Condor, breaking off a wing. The Condor turned on its back and dived into the sea, amid audible cheers from the whole convoy. The Hurricane pilot decided to make for Loch Earn, Scotland, some 300 miles away, where he landed safely. The Hurricane pilot, Lt Robert Everett, was later awarded a DSO for shooting down a Condor, after which episode he ditched in the sea. / Drawing by John Scott.

Interlude in Russia

Hurricanes took part in a unique episode during the war. They were the only weapon used by British personnel to engage the enemy alongside members of the Russian armed forces.

This action took place towards the end of 1941, when Britain decided to send Russia as much material aid as possible to help the hard-pressed Red Army.

An important part of this aid was to comprise Hurricanes, and to train Russian personnel how to erect, maintain and operate the fighters, a new Wing, No 151, was formed at Leconfield in August. An Expedition, comprising Nos 81 and 134 Squadrons, with 39 Hurricane MarkIIBs, and their pilots and ground crews, assembled as follows:

Twenty-four Hurricanes embarked in flying trim on HMS *Argus,* the remaining 15 being crated and stowed as deck cargo on other ships. The ground crews and remaining pilots embarked on the SS *Llanstephan Castle.* Setting sail on August 21st the convoy arrived off Murmansk on the 28th. Here the 24 Hurricanes flew off the *Argus* and landed at Vianga, an airfield about 15 miles away which was to be the Wing's main base during its stay in Russia.

Enemy air activity, however, prevented the remainder of the convoy from being unloaded and it sailed further east to Archangel. This effectively split the British force; the fighters which landed at Vianga being without ground crews or supplies, and the personnel at Archangel with full supplies and crates of Hurricanes, but without the normal facilities for assembly.

The main body of the force then started what turned out to be a highly adventurous trip from Archangel to Murmansk by rail, while others went by air and sea. The party remaining started to uncrate and assemble the Hurricanes. These had been dumped haphazardly in an uneven-lying mud flat, so that each crate presented a particular problem in getting its aircraft into the neighbouring hangar. A major snag was the discovery that most of the special tools required for assembly, the propeller and sparking plug spanners among them, were missing. However, the Russians had gathered together an extremely capable body of technicians to undergo instruction, as in their turn they would be passing on their knowledge to countless others, and they worked wonders in not only improvising the tools required, but also other parts. For example, when it was discovered that the gun blast tubes would not fit—these having been taken from Hurricane Mark Is—the Russians in one evening drew up and made in local workshops enough blast tube adapters for the entire Wing. With this sort of enthusiasm the small British detachment was able to assemble and fly the 15 Hurricanes in nine days.

A secondary duty of the Wing, more spectacular though less basic, was to demonstrate the destructive

qualities of the 12-gun Hurricane in action. In other words, to shoot down enemy aircraft.

This was easier hoped for than achieved. Being some 170 miles inside the Arctic Circle, the 'days' comprised little more than two or three hours of daylight.

During one patrol on September 11th the pilots of two aircraft of No 134 Squadron had narrow escapes when their engines cut out several times—as a result of the Russian petrol. This happened while they were over enemy occupied territory and only when they were within a few hundred feet of the ground did their energetic operation of the priming pump bring life back to the Merlins—and the pilots back to base.

Success came the following day when five Hurricanes of No 81 Squadron went into action against five Messerschmitt Bf109Es escorting a Henschel Hs126. Three Bf109s were shot down and the Hs126 damaged, for the loss of one Hurricane. The pilot lost during this engagement was the only one of the Wing to lose his life throughout its stay in Russia.

Further successes were achieved the following day when eight Hurricanes of the same Squadron took off to escort some Russian bombers returning to base. Eight

Left: Hurricanes of No 151 Wing in Russia returning to their base after a patrol during which they escorted Red Air Force bombers over enemy lines. During between 30 and 40 such escort patrols the Wing never lost a Russian bomber. Russian crews became so confident when escorted by the Hurricanes that they ceased bothering to look overhead.

Below: This photograph, and those on the following page, give a good idea of the extremely bitter conditions in which the Hurricanes fought in Russia. The tropical filter on this MarkIIB is evidence of the aircraft's original Middle East destination.

Bf109Es were sighted preparing to attack the bombers and the Hurricanes went for them. The CO fired at one, hitting its radiator, and then chased it for about five minutes, using up all his ammunition. The Bf109 was then attacked by two more Hurricanes after which it crashed. Another Hurricane pilot made a stern attack on a second Bf109, without visible success, until a lucky oblique shot set the enemy aircraft on fire. Yet another Hurricane pilot out-turned a Bf109, and then despatched it with two short, well-aimed bursts of fire.

In the five or six days during which full contact with the enemy was possible by offensive-patrols, 15 German aircraft were shot down for certain and many others damaged, for the loss of only one Hurricane.

The fifteen-to-one claim is so big as to imply either gross exaggeration or over enthusiasm on the part of the Hurricane pilots. The care with which claims were investigated, however, is indicated by the following single example. This procedure is also relevant to the Battle of Britain Postscript regarding claims and recorded losses during that Battle. The example is told by Flt Lt Hubert Griffith who accompanied the Wing to Russia:

'Late one afternoon, "B" Flight, 81 Squadron, had come down from a patrol, claiming three victories. Two of these were unquestionable. There was no possible doubt about them. They had been seen by independent witnesses to crash into the ground, and the wrecks had been identified. About the third there was a dispute. The young Scottish pilot who had engaged the third aircraft swore that he had got to close quarters, had squirted his 12 guns into it in a long, close-range burst of fire, and had only desisted when he had seen the enemy machine go down in an out-of-control spin in a cloud near the ground. His story was confirmed, in detail, by his flight-commander, a pilot of long experience. But it was the Squadron Leader, a pilot of even greater experience, who had to give the decision on what claim to put in to Intelligence, and his comment on hearing the story was: "Yes . . . but they can take an awful lot of lead and still get away with it; we'll only have to claim him a 'probable.'"

'The encounter then, was entered in the records as a "probable," and the matter could have finished there. It was only the next morning, when the wreckage of the third enemy machine had been definitely identified on the ground, that the claim was allowed to go forward as a certain victory.'

In addition to the offensive patrols, the Wing flew many flights escorting Russian bombers. Towards the end of their stay this was their main task, and gave the Russian bomber crews complete confidence. One bomber pilot stated: 'When the Hurricanes are escorting us, we never even bother to look up overhead. We concentrate on going straight to our objectives.' During all the escort patrols, between 30 and 40, the Wing never lost a Russian bomber.

The first Russian to fly a Hurricane was the Air Officer Commanding, General Kuznetsov. The second was Captain Safonov.

So quick were the Russians in learning to service and maintain the Hurricane, that by November, 1941, the Wing was able to hand over its aircraft to the 72nd

Regiment of the Red Naval Air Fleet who formed their first Hurricane Wing, of three Squadrons, commanded by Safonov, now promoted to Colonel. Their tasks done, the personnel of No 151 Wing RAF embarked for home.

Subsequently many more hundreds of Hurricanes were delivered to Russia, until, ultimately, the total reached 2,952. This is more than one-fifth of all the Hurricanes produced.

Details of the use to which they were put are not easy to come by. It is known that the Russians carried out a number of interesting modifications. Several two-seaters were evolved, one with a dorsal gun position. Because of the large numbers of American fighters armed with 0.50in machine-guns supplied to Russia, a number of the Hurricanes were adapted to mount this calibre of gun.

One of the few accounts of the Hurricane's service on the Russian front appeared in the *Soviet War News* issue of October 3rd, 1942, from which the following extracts are taken:—

'Then a batch of English Hawker Hurricane fighters arrived at the Front. The speeds for which these machines are designed suggested that they would be particularly suitable as escorts for the Ilyushin bombers. Their excellent lateral manoeuvrability promised a solution to the problem of low-level fighters. It was therefore decided to employ Hurricanes to escort the Il bombers. For about three months now Major Gorshkov's unit of Hurricanes has been escorting your fighter-bombers on their sorties. His airmen have splendid victories to their credit.

'On one occasion, six Hurricanes were detailed to accompany eight Il aircraft. The Group Leader, Lieutenant Dobrovolsky, decided against dividing his forces, preferring to keep them in the immediate vicinity of the bombers, the better to ensure their protection. Over the target they were met by eight Messerchmitts. The bombers were flying at an altitude of 1,300 feet, and they immediately formed into a circle. Among them the Hurricanes were busy keeping the enemy busy. After a few minutes, Dobrovolsky set fire to one Messerschmitt, then Sergeants Barishnyov and Bunakov each made a kill. While this fight was going on, the bombers, without breaking their circle, continued to strafe the troop concentrations. When they ran out of bombs they veered round in a wide sweep and started on their return journey. This fight ended in the complete defeat of the German airmen, who, after losing three of their aircraft, were forced to give up the attack. Such tactics are now common practice among Soviet pilots and they have brought excellent results. In three months' hard work, the Il bombers have suffered one loss from attacks by enemy fighters. The quality of the Hurricane has made it possible for us to solve the important problem of ensuring the safety of the Il.

'The British machines have proved equally successful on reconnaissance duty and in guarding troops and military objectives. For over two months past, Major Panov's unit has been flying Hurricanes. With some 20 machines at his disposal, his unit has brought down 83 German 'planes in aerial combat, including 31 bombers, and this for the price of only four pilots and ten 'planes.'

WITH THE ROYAL AIR FORCE IN RUSSIA

Above left: Hurricane in Russia. Over 2,950 Hurricanes were supplied to Russia, a fifth of the total number built. The first fifteen aircraft were assembled by a British working party at Archangel. Initially members of this erection party were billeted in an ancient river paddle steamer reminiscent of the one in Mark Twain's 'Life on the Mississippi.' Nicknamed the 'winkle-barge' the lower deck was abandoned after one night because of the reception given to the inmates by a particularly vicious brash of bugs.

Top: During its three-month stay in Russia, No 151 Wing, in addition to instructing Russian personnel, shot down fifteen enemy aircraft for the loss of only one Hurricane. For each victory the British pilots qualified for a bonus of 100 roubles (about £20 at that time) from the Soviet authorities. The money was refused by the Hurricane pilots who stated it would spoil their 'amateur status.' Ultimately, the money was collected in bulk and transferred to the RAF Benevolent Fund.

Above: Several British personnel had narrow escapes during an enemy raid on the No 151 Wing base at Vianga, near Murmansk. The Engineer Officer was blown clear across the repair workshop, but was uninjured. One flight mechanic got a chip out of his shin. One pilot was actually taking off when a bomb landed right in front of his aircraft, stopping the engine. The pilot climbed out on the wing of his machine — and was then promptly blown off by the blast of another bomb into a muddy puddle. Apart from his dignity, he was unhurt.

Left: Typical 'grainy' Russian photograph, one of the few official pictures released showing a Hurricane in Red Air Force markings. Many of the Hurricanes, diverted to Russia at short notice, arrived with Royal Air Force markings. With the minimum of ceremony, and not bothering to paint these out completely, the Russians merely superimposed their red star on the roundels.

Hurricane Specials

In view of the undoubted versatility of the Hurricane, it is, perhaps, surprising that the airframe was not developed in the traditional sense. Throughout its life span there was really only one basic version, unless one considers that the installation of the more powerful Merlin XX, with its two-stage supercharger, produced a new variant. The reason for this is that there was no need to, as Spitfires were available to undertake many of the special duties for which the Hurricane could have been developed.

As with most basically sound aircraft, however, a large number of 'special' Hurricanes were studied. Many of these remained projects on paper, but some reached the hardware stage.

One of the most unusual developments was the 'slip-wing' Hurricane. Known officially as the Hillson FH40, this involved fitting an extra top wing, so turning it into a biplane, as a means of providing extra lift for take-off from very small airfields. Once the Hurricane was airborne, the extra wing was to be jettisoned, together with the interplane struts. An early Hurricane I, L1884, was chosen for the experiment. Several flights were made in the biplane configuration, before the scheme was abandoned in 1943. Also aimed at producing a Hurricane capable of operating from small airfields, at overload weights, was the special Hurricane II experimentally equipped with take-off rockets.

In addition to the main production lines in England, a second European source of supply of Hurricanes was established in Belgium, by Avions Fairey, which in August 1939 had received a contract to build 80 of the fighters. Of interest is that these Hurricanes were 'specials' in that they were to be armed with four heavy 12.7mm FN Browning machine-guns instead of the normal eight 0.303in guns.

By May 10th, 1940, one aircraft had been delivered to Evere airfield, a second machine had been flown by test pilot Eyskens, a third was ready for tests and several were nearing completion, when the German invasion began and the works were bombed.

Early 1941 had seen the production of a Hurricane 'Special' in Yugoslavia. To prepare for a separate source of power plants, and to provide a comparison for performance and handling, the Yugoslavs fitted a 1,050hp Daimler-Benz DB601A engine in place of the Rolls-Royce Merlin. Some Yugoslav pilots are reported to have preferred the Daimler-Benz-engined version, but it is unlikely that any trials conducted would have been truly comparative. This Hurricane really deserves the appellation special, as it is thought to be the only one ever to have flown with an engine other than the Merlin.

A 'Special' which did not quite come off, or rather which was not quite completed, was an invention born of necessity through the German invasion of Norway. With this attack the Wehrmacht had moved overseas—and was thus dependent on seaborne supplies. These could be

Above left: The Hillson FH40 'slip wing' Hurricane. This was a Mark I aircraft, L1884, modified to take the experimental top wing. The purpose of the scheme was to provide extra lift to enable the Hurricane to take off from smaller fields. After becoming airborne, the top wing would be jettisoned.

Left: A fine photograph of an early Yugoslav Hurricane, flown by Hawker Test Pilot Philip Lucas. An initial order for twelve machines was received in 1938, followed by a second order for twelve and an application to build the fighter under licence in Yugoslavia. The twenty-four Hawker-built aircraft and twenty licence-built in Yugoslavia had been delivered to the Royal Yugoslav Air Force, before German forces overran the country in April, 1941.

Above: A Hurricane with — according to the original caption on the back of the photograph — 'snow feet.' It is, in fact, a Canadian Hurricane XII, No 5624, fitted with an experimental ski undercarriage to permit operations from snow-covered airfields.

strangled, thought the British High Command, by the Royal Navy and the re-conquest of Norway begun. Little, however, could be done without command of the air. Thus, a fighter was needed urgently, one that could use the innumerable lakes and fjords of that country. At worst such an aircraft would gain some relief for the British troops committed to the battle.

Accordingly, it was decided to try and equip a Hurricane with floats so that it could be operated as a floatplane. There was no time to design an optimised pair of floats and it was decided to use a pair from a Blackburn Roc. These were, in fact, too big and unsuitable from the start, but work pressed on. In order to reduce drag to a minimum much ingenuity was displayed in the design of the inter-connecting structure.

The wing centre section had been mated with the float structure when the Norwegian campaign ended and the project was abandoned.

One of the most interesting Hurricane 'Specials' is of particular interest to the writer, because, as a young draughtsman working in the Hawker Design Office during the war under the stern but wise guidance of the late Sir Sydney Camm, I prepared the necessary drawings. At the time the installation was so secret that the project was given the code-name 'Sunflower Seed.' After a search extending over a quarter of a century I have not yet been able to locate a photograph of the Hurricane in question! An artist's impression, however, appears in the central colour section of this book.

The object was to determine whether it was practical to fire rockets vertically from aircraft, to counter enemy aircraft from dropping bombs on formations of Allied bombers.

The Hurricane installation consisted of a simple tube, about 6in in diameter, mounted behind the cockpit, with the open ends protruding above and below the fuselage.

For the first live test, if my memory serves me, the pilot wore an army-type tin helmet and flew with the normal sliding hood removed, as this would have fouled the tube projecting up through the fuselage behind the cockpit. The first test rocket fired severely damaged the fairing around the tube. The damage, however, was soon repaired and the area locally protected by duralumin sheeting, after which further firings were made satisfactorily even if rather frighteningly. The idea was not adopted on a large scale.

With the object of delivering fighters direct from Britain to Malta by air and of providing air protection for convoys far out to sea, or for long-range bombing missions, four Hurricanes were used in 1941 in towing trials behind Wellingtons. The idea was that should the need arise the Hurricane would be released, start its engine, and be ready to engage the enemy. The trials showed that prolonged towing resulted in the Hurricane icing up, making it difficult, if not impossible, to start the engine.

Similar motives led to a proposal for a Hurricane-Liberator composite aircraft, the Hurricane being mounted on top of the Liberator and released on the

approach of enemy aircraft. Trials indicated the Hurricane would ice up, making it difficult to start the engine and this idea, together with that for towed Hurricanes, was dropped.

The return of peace and the obvious superiority of jet propelled fighter aircraft combined to restrict the development of post-war 'Specials.'

However, one 'Special' which did not see the light of day until after the war, was the Persian Hurricane IIC two-seater trainer. With the end of the war Hawkers began their traditional quest for foreign orders. The first customer was Portugal—Britain's oldest ally—and the second Persia, who placed an order for 16 Hurricanes. This Persian post-war order was in fact intended to complete a pre-war order for 18 aircraft placed in 1939 of which only two had been delivered before the outbreak of large scale hostilities.

The Persian two-seat trainer was based largely on drawings prepared in 1940 for a similar project designed and almost completed for the Royal Air Force. The second pilot was located immediately behind the existing cockpit, little modification to the basic structure being necessary. The top fuselage stringers were terminated about four feet further aft and extra cross members inserted between the longerons. Initially both the front and rear cockpits were uncovered, the front position being protected by the

Above: Persian two-seat trainer fitted with a sliding hood, adapted from a Tempest canopy, over the rear cockpit. It was in this form that the Hurricanes were delivered to Doshan Teppeh in 1947.

Left: Two-seat Persian Hurricane trainer. It is shown here in its original form with its uncomfortable and draughty open rear cockpit.

Below: At dispersal! A fine study of the remarkable 5/8-scale flying model of the Hurricane made by Fred Sindlinger.

normal windscreen and frame, and the rear position by only a simple transparent fairing. However, tests indicated that the rear position was extremely draughty, and a fairing was added together with a Tempest-type sliding hood. The machine, which had a top speed of 320mph, was delivered in 1947.

Perhaps less dramatic but probably more useful was Z3687, an early Hurricane which was fitted with a special Armstrong Whitworth laminar-flow wing of reduced thickness-to-chord ratio, and flight tested at Farnborough.

The most unusual of all the special Hurricanes, however, is not a Hurricane at all—or is it? This 'Special' is a remarkable five-eighths full-size scale replica of the Hurricane made by Fred Sindlinger of Puyallup, Washington. The 25-foot wing span replica is accurately scaled down in almost every detail. The cockpit area is about 4 inches out of scale in both width and height, but in practice it is only the engine cowling, which encloses a 150hp Lycoming driving a Hartzell constant-speed propeller, which gives the game away, and then only to experts.

Enthusiast Sindlinger built nearly everything himself, except the engine, propeller, wheels and tyres.

With people like Fred Sindlinger around who can say that even now we have seen the last of the Hurricane Specials!

Hurricane Restoration

Although a very large number of Hurricanes—over 14,000—was built, only three airworthy examples survive today. It was, therefore, an event of no little historical significance when the then two survivors were joined by a third one in June, 1973. The event occurred at Strathallan Castle, between Perth and Stirling, in the heart of Scotland.

The story starts in 1970 when Sir William J. D. Roberts, a private pilot since 1957 and farmer, was attracted by the Hurricane which was being offered for sale together with two Spitfire IXs. Willie Roberts, as everybody seems to call him, thought that this rare British fighter should be preserved in Britain. Thus germinated his idea of the Strathallan Collection museum of Second World War piston-engined aircraft. Currently, in addition to the Hurricane, the Collection impressively includes four Spitfires, three TMkIXs and one MkXIV, a Blenheim IV, a Fairey Battle, a Lockheed Hudson, a Mosquito, a Lysander, an Anson, a Harvard, a Tiger Moth and a Puss Moth.

As far as the Hurricane acquisition is concerned Willie Roberts commented 'The Hurricane is a very British aircraft and I wanted to preserve one. It is more appealing to me than the Spitfire—more robust and solid. It was the underdog in the Battle of Britain, but it shot down more enemy aircraft. A lot of people have forgotten that. And there's no sound like the sound of Merlins. It makes you feel proud to be British.'

Negotiations to purchase the Hurricane extended over four months, but this merely presaged three years' hard work. In some respects the task of restoration was similar to that of renovating a vintage car, but with one vital difference. Engineering ability and enthusiasm are needed for both ventures. On a car, enthusiasm is often more valuable than engineering ability; on an aircraft, however, enthusiasm alone could bring irresponsibility; engineering considerations must take first place.

If a fuel pump fails on a newly restored car, the only casualty is the red face of the driver; onlookers are usually delighted. The possible consequences of a fuel pump failing on the Hurricane while over a built-up area, however, are obvious.

The small team of engineers involved on the Hurricane were greatly assisted in their formidable task by the availability of a set of production drawings and copies of all the Royal Air Force technical Air Publications issued for the fighter.

At the start of the restoration the aircraft was very thoroughly torn apart and the following work carried out. All timbers and fabric were renewed throughout. The flying control cables were all replaced with new items. All the fuel and oil tanks were overhauled and pressure checked. All the instruments were overhauled. While the airframe was stripped, the structure was X-rayed. All the

electrical wiring was renewed and all the electrical components overhauled or renewed.

No insurmountable problems were encountered during the rebuild, but careful planning and workmanship were continuous requirements. Two items which emphasise this were the rebuilding of the fuselage timber formers to the correct contours and the fuselage fuel tank installation. The original tank mounting stirrups had long since corroded away, which meant designing a platform of sufficient strength to accept the loading of 35 gallons of fuel both structurally and under the required 'g' loading, and cunningly shaped to avoid the myriad of 'bits and pieces' which abound in this area, while still maintaining the strength required. The platform was fabricated from 6 swg duralumin and the tank retained by stainless steel straps which run right over the tank, and are tensioned by turnbuckles attached to the platform.

Even the lesser jobs required plenty of painstaking effort and ingenuity. In spite of this—or rather because of it—the project was a source of great satisfaction to all those engaged on it.

All told over 5,000 man hours were expended on the restoration to get the aircraft airworthy. The team was not, of course, engaged on the Hurricane exclusively; they did have other commitments.

The first post-restoration flight was made on June 28th, 1973, at the experienced hands of Duncan Simpson, chief test pilot at HSA. Kingston, whose normal job is flying Hunters or Harriers. There was only one cause for momentary concern during the flight—an unfamiliar smell. This was the varnish protecting the gleaming polished copper coolant pipes running through the cockpit.

Above: Strathallan Hurricane. Built originally by the Canadian Car and Foundry Company, Ontario, in late 1942, the Hurricane, a MarkIIB and powered by a Packard Merlin 29, entered service with the RCAF, with which it served from November 1942 to October 1952. Then, with only 87 hours in the log-book, it was bought as scrap by a farmer for his children to play with. In 1964 it was bought by Robert Diemert and rebuilt in 1966 at Friendship Field when it was fitted with a Merlin 224. It flew 80 hours while the 'Battle of Britain' film was being made. The current engine is a Merlin 25, acquired from a Spanish Air Force Heinkel He111.

Above right: Hurricane pride. Sir William Roberts, of Strathallan Castle, private pilot and farmer (right) and the team of engineers responsible for restoring the Hurricane, shortly after the first post-restoration flight. From left to right: Duncan Simpson, HSA Dunsfold, chief test pilot; Bert Hayward and G. 'Mac' Miller, HSA Dunsfold engineers; David Lawson, Dick Richardson, Jim Hutchinson and Jim Smith, Strathallan Collection engineers.

Right: A view of the Hurricane during an early stage of restoration.

The Making of a Fighter

Below: Checking the alignment of an engine bearer.

Right: Checking the engagement of a retracted undercarriage leg with its locking mechanism. Note the two self-sealing fuel tanks in the centre section.

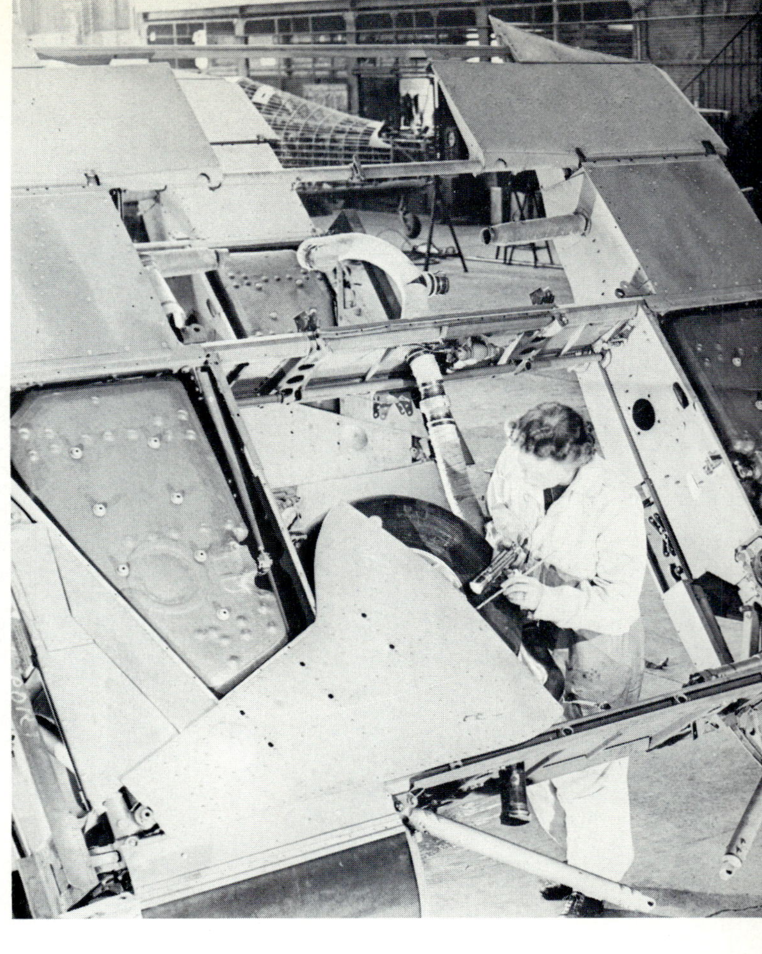

Left: Preparing to cover the fuselage with canvas. An ingenious method was used to secure the fabric. Certain stringers had a channel in their outer edge across which the canvas was laid and secured by a U-section member fitted into the channel and secured by screws. A fabric strip was doped over the channel to give a smooth finish. In this way the loads were distributed along the whole length of each stringer and not merely applied at a series of points.

Above right: With the fuselage completed and the engine installed, the wings are placed in position ready for mating with the centre section.

Right: Hurricane MarkIICs on the production line at Langley. This new factory at Parlaunt Farm, completed in 1939, was the main production centre for Hurricanes, turning out over 7,000 machines. The other major Hurricane production centre was the Gloster Aircraft works at Brockworth, which turned out 2,749 aircraft. One production batch of 300 was built by the Austin Motor Co. at their Longbridge plant during 1941. A total of 1,077 Hurricanes, powered by Packard-built Merlins, were built by the Canadian Car and Foundry Corporation, Canada.

Far right: Complete except for spinner and cowling panels, last minute adjustments and checks are made.

Last of the Many

The last of over 14,000 Hurricanes—PZ865—came off the production line at Langley in August, 1944. It was never issued to the Royal Air Force, being purchased by Hawker Aircraft from the Ministry of Aircraft Production. Appropriately named *The Last of the Many*, it was rolled out at a special ceremony held to commemorate its completion, when it was displayed together with a vintage Hawker Hart biplane—its 'grandfather'—and a Tempest —its 'grandson.' On this happy occasion PZ865 was flown by 'George' Bulman, Hawker test pilot who, ten years earlier, had guided the Hurricane prototype through its initial trials.

The Last of the Many has had a colourful history. When peace returned, it was placed on the civil register as G-AMAU. It was de-armed by the removal of the guns and painted a brilliant royal blue and gold.

In 1950 it was displayed at the Royal Aeronautical Society Garden Party. It next appeared in the King's Cup Race where, entered by HRH Princess Margaret, it gained second place. In August, 1950, it flew in the Kemsby Trophy Race at Fairwood Common, when it came third at an average speed of ·295mph. In 1951 it was again displayed at the RAeS Garden Party, and again took part in the National Air Races. In that year G-AMAU also starred in two war films—*Hawks in the Sun* and in *Angels one five*—in which it was repainted to represent a Battle of Britain machine. 1952 saw the aircraft at a Vintage Rally. 1953 at the Garden Party. 1954 in the National Air Races. 1955 at the RAE Jubilee Display.

In 1960 the decision was taken to restore the aircraft to its original camouflage scheme, although the civil registration was retained. The aircraft is now thought to be unique in bearing simultaneously both civil and military registrations.

During the nineteen sixties it became popular for Hawker pilots to use the aircraft for taxi purposes. Nor were its duties all pleasure. During target towing trials on the Sea Fury for the Germans it was pressed into service as a 'chase plane.' During the early transition trials with the Hawker P1127 vertical take-off aircraft—forerunner of the world famous Harrier—*The Last of the Many* was again used as a chase plane, because of its exceptional speed range.

Thus, this story of the Hurricane draws to a close. But the memory of this truly great British fighter will continue as long as there are books on aircraft.

The 'Last of the Many,' with its guns removed and repainted in its original camouflage scheme. It bears both the Service No PZ865 and, under the tailplane, the civil registration G-AMAU.